Count Your Blessings:
Colin's Story

Hazel Barker

Count Your Blessings: Colin's Story

© Hazel Barker 2020

Published by Armour Books
P. O. Box 492, Corinda QLD 4075, Australia

Photo credits:

puruan | istockphoto bicycle icon
tsvibrav | istockphoto Cape Nelson lighthouse
Mario Rui Andre | unsplash bicycle at the beach

ISBN: 978-1-925380-30-9

A catalogue record for this book is available from the National Library of Australia

No part of this book may be reproduced, stored in a retrieval system or transmitted in any form or by any means, without the prior permission in writing of the publisher, nor be otherwise circulated in any form of binding or cover other than that in which it is published and without a similar condition, including this condition, being imposed on the subsequent purchaser.

Note: Australian spelling and grammatical conventions are used throughout this book.

Endorsements

The narrative is compelling. The voice of the narrator is warm, and the plot unfolds naturally. The structure is sound, with the right balance of sensory memories and plot turning points.

The mother's anger and mood swings are both terrifying and compelling. We really feel for the child protagonist and his tendon operation. A sick child always provides high stakes. There is no one more vulnerable than a child and no death worse than a child's.

Good luck with it. It is a gorgeous memoir.

—*Sandra Thidodeaux*
Lecturer in Literary Studies and Creative Writing,
Charles Darwin University

I enjoyed reading *Count Your Blessings*. It is well written and full of beautiful imagery.

—*Kathy Stewart*
Editor, Authors' Ally
and author of over 16 books

You have taken on a difficult task, telling your husband's story in your own words. You and Colin have such a wonderful relationship and are very close.

—*Margaret Dakin*
Playwright and author of several
award-winning short stories

Also by Hazel Barker

Heaven Tempers the Wind: Story of a War Child
Finalist CALEB Awards 2017

The Sides of Heaven
Finalist CALEB Awards 2019

The Chocolate Soldier: Story of a Conchie.

Acknowledgements

Sincere thanks to members of my writing groups, and special thanks to Kathy Stewart and Margaret Dakin for beta reading *Count Your Blessings*.

My thanks also to the Redland Libraries for their support in launching my books and for their encouragement to all local authors.

Thanks also, to the Logan, Gold Coast and Sunshine Coast libraries for giving me the opportunity to speak at their libraries and promote my books.

My heartfelt gratitude to my husband Colin, who shared his life story with me and allowed me to ghost-write his wonderful adventures.

Finally, I wish to thank my publisher, Armour Books, who discovered me when I first entered the world of writing.

This book is dedicated

to my husband

Colin Richard Barker,

who shared with me

the story of his life.

Without him,

this story could not have been written.

Contents

Chapter 1 .... page 11
Chapter 2 .... page 17
Chapter 3 .... page 23
Chapter 4 .... page 31
Chapter 5 .... page 39
Chapter 6 .... page 47
Chapter 7 .... page 59
Chapter 8 .... page 67
Chapter 9 .... page 73
Chapter 10 .... page 83
Chapter 11 .... page 95
Chapter 12 .... page 105
Chapter 13 .... page 115
Chapter 14 .... page 125
Chapter 15 .... page 133
Chapter 16 .... page 143
Chapter 17 .... page 151
Chapter 18 .... page 157

Foreword

I have written this story because I want posterity to know of a way of life that helped shape Australian history. I would like to add to the tapestry of world history and leave a trail for people to follow and learn that life is not a bed of roses but a journey through happiness and sorrow.

Chapter 1

MINE WAS A SOLITARY CHILDHOOD. I remember nothing of Sherwood Forest's great oaks even though, I, Colin Barker, came from Robin Hood country. Dad, Mum and I had left England when I was only two. I can recall my grandfather's black face. My grandfather, Harold, worked the coalface at Gedling pit, Nottingham. I vaguely recollect sitting on the lap of a big, black man. I had never known him except as the 'black' man who was forever spitting into his handkerchief. So black, even his spit was black.

'One for you and one for me,' he'd say, taking a spoonful of food into his mouth—a huge hole like the cavities he carved in the coal face. After the meal, the house would resound with his strong baritone voice singing the old songs of yesteryear.

We lived in my grandfather's home because houses were scarce in post-war England. Dad applied for a Council house but had to wait his turn.

'And anyway, didn't you know there's been a war?' the clerk replied when Dad had grumbled at the long wait.

Dad fumed. 'After fighting for king and country for four years, I've been placed at the bottom of the list!'

We sailed from Southampton as ten-pound Poms in 1948, because Dad had been out of work for sixteen weeks. I remember the day we crossed the Equator when passengers gathered at the ship's rail. Sailors fished an old man out of the ocean. He wore a beard, had a crown on his head and a pitchfork in his hand. Garlanded with seaweed, he roared and chased everyone, leaving behind a pool of water and paper streamers. He especially targeted the children.

I clung to Mum's dress and wouldn't let go until he'd gone.

She said, 'He's King Neptune. He won't hurt you.'

Neptune had frightened me so much that I joined the others and clapped when he left.

On our arrival in Melbourne, Australia, we stayed for a while with our distant relatives from England before moving to Portland, Victoria, where Dad found work as a bricklayer on the construction of the Wool Appraisal Complex.

We lived in a large wooden structure on the site, a few miles from the town centre and shared a community bathroom, kitchen and dining room. Mum cooked for the workers, many of whom were migrants. There were also some Australians. To amuse myself, I'd climb in and out of the empty wool crates, popping up like a jack-in-the-box until I grew tired. Then I'd join my parents and listen to the adults talking.

One of my earliest memories of Portland was the time Mum had gone shopping and left me alone on the beach. Looking back now, I think she may have asked a friend to keep an eye on me. I recall the sun shining on the glittering sand and the wind sighing in the distant hills, in sympathy with my loneliness. Jasmine entwined itself around the trees, birds lifted their heads, throats moving in unison like choirs of angels, warbling a greeting to their Creator. A breeze wafted its strong fragrance towards me. I licked my lips and tasted the salty flavour of the sea. The sea that would have such an influence on my life. The sea that would calm me in moments of anxiety. The sea, whose voice I could not still.

Mum's words kept ringing in my ears. 'Now Colin, I'll be gone for just a little while. Wait for me here and don't get dirty. Don't play in the sand.'

My mother's warning whirled around my head like a spinning top. They blotted out everything. The waves stopped lapping on the beach, the trees became still, the birds ceased singing. I remained glued to the spot as if mesmerised. In my imagination, I built castles with my red bucket and spade. Some small. Others reaching up forever. The soft summer breeze rippled my hair like a caress. I licked the salty flavour on my lips.

Time passed. I don't recall how long Mum was away. Was it minutes or hours?

On her return, arms laden with shopping, holding out a peppermint cane wrapped in cellophane. 'Here's something for you.' Her blue eyes gazed into mine, and her blonde hair shone in the sunlight.

I murmured my thanks and tore off the wrapping, sucking and licking in an ecstasy of delight. I never knew what to expect from Mum. Some days she'd hug me and call me endearing names. On bad days, she'd give my ear a resounding box and say, 'Go away and be quiet.'

Like all artists, I had my own three-legged easel. I can never forget the day I'd completed a beautiful drawing on a slate with coloured chalk. Proud of my work, I ran over to the kitchen, saying, 'Mummy, Mummy. Look at my picture.'

'Go away. I'm busy now,' she shouted and, taking the slate, threw it against the wall.

It smashed.

Humiliated by the sharp rebuff, I raced into the bedroom, picked up Heffalump and buried my face in his. The elephant was blue with a patchwork saddle. I called him Heffalump because Dad had read me stories of Christopher Robin and his woodland friends. Now, my dear friend's long trunk entwined my neck, as sobs shook my body. Eyes heavy with unshed tears, I locked my arms locked around him. A painful lump rose in my throat, strangling me. I clenched my teeth to prevent the sobs from escaping.

Whenever Mum yelled at me, I would withdrew within myself and repress all emotions. Shyness enveloped me like a coat-of-armour. Nothing could penetrate its protective cover.

As soon as the Wool Appraisal Building was completed, Dad rented a house about two miles out of town. It stood on a hill and had an excellent view. The steep cliffs to the north contrasted sharply with the sandy beaches off Dutton Way on the south. I would gaze out from the window of my bedroom, enjoying the fresh salty air. The waves rolled and curved in a long arch, then fell with spurts of foam. When the southerlies blew, the sea turned into a mass of mountains and the waves slapped against the cliffs like thunder.

On the horizon, sometimes obscured by clouds and mist, the sea held Julia Percy Island in its embrace. The big, sandy bay, on the mainland, appeared to touch the island in some places and I often tried to get to it but no matter how far I walked along the beach, the further away it seemed.

Fishermen said, 'The island shelters rabbits of all colours within its womb—white, brown, grey, or black.'

Their words increased my love and longing for the island.

Our house was next to a cemetery and, because I grew restless when confined indoors, Mum allowed me to play there. In winter, cold winds would blow, funnelling through the avenues of stone memorials. Large pin oaks littered the ground with their needles. A perfect sylvan nook, it was steeped in solitude and shaded from the sun. Only the screeching gulls overhead or the waves breaking on the seashore, shattered the silence. The ground had small mounds and I'd play with my wooden truck, happy and carefree among the old tombstones. Some of them bent forward, as though weighed down by their past sins.

Fortunately, none of the old and cracked monuments fell and crushed my skull like an eggshell. At times, I'd feel an inhuman presence moving among the pines. I particularly felt the presence of another boy a bit older than myself, who joined me in my games.

In the evenings, I'd relate my adventures to Dad, just as Christopher Robin did in the book, Pooh Bear. He would listen carefully, at times punctuating my talk with a hearty laugh.

My parents made certain I'd never forget my roots. They pored over pictures of Nottingham and its famous buildings. 'The stone for constructing the Council House came from the same quarry as St Paul's Cathedral in London,' Dad said, with a gleam in his eyes.

Whenever my parents reminisced about Nottingham's Goose Fair, I'd imagine a sea of geese. Geese charging people with their long necks stuck out like swords, honking and drowning all other noise. Geese—a mass of white heads and flapping wings.

I have a vivid recollection of my childhood days in Portland. I recall strolling through clumps of flowers and hearing the rustle of leaves or the laugh of a kookaburra. I loved wandering around Daffodil Farm where beds of white and yellow flowers spread across the alluvial lands. The yellow blooms on their green stalks, all dancing in time to the breeze, would bring Goose Fair to my mind.

Just before my fifth birthday, Mum said, 'You're growing up so fast, your tendons won't grow as quickly as the rest of your body.'

I had no idea what tendons were. All I knew was that I walked on tip-toes. It affected my balance and added to my bashfulness.

'I'm taking you to Doctor Kneebone.' Mum said. 'He's a specialist, who practises in Hamilton. You'll love Hamilton.'

I thought it funny that a surgeon with a name like Kneebone was to operate on my foot. Perhaps his name should have been Legbone or Anklebone!

Portland did not have many facilities, and a visit to a doctor entailed a bus ride to Hamilton, some sixty miles away. I looked forward to a wonderful holiday and chirped with joy all the way to hospital.

On the day of the operation, a nurse lifted me up to the window. 'Look at the farmlands. They're so fresh and green.'

She gave me a bath in a huge white tub with sides that towered above me. The water was warm, with bubbly soap and the slippery, soothing sensation calmed my racing heart. At home, I had nothing but the kitchen sink to bathe in, and the towel was rough and scratchy. Now I had soft fluffy towels.

Another nurse said, 'I'm taking you for a ride on a trolley.' She put me on a narrow bed, and wheeled me into a room with bright lights. So bright, I could hardly see anything.

'Breathe in deeply,' she whispered, as if telling me a secret. Then she slipped something on my nose.

This must be how horses feel with a nosebag on, I thought, before drifting off.

I can't recall any pain. My legs remained in plaster casts for some time after the operation. I wore boots with two steel rods on either side, during the day. They made walking difficult, but Mum and Dad fussed over me.

'They're called callipers,' Mum said. 'You wear them because you're special.'

Chapter 2

MUM ENROLLED ME AT SCHOOL when I turned six. I didn't mind the idea too much at first, because Dad spoke of school in glowing terms. Then I thought of my callipers and my mind verged on panic.

My apprehension became unbearable from the minute we entered the school grounds and everyone stared. Once Mum had left, they laughed at me. Some called out, 'Cripple,' and others joined in, shouting 'Peg-leg.'

At playtime, they shoved and pushed me until I lost balance and fell. Some imitated my clumsy run. Screaming with derision, they ran straight-legged, swinging their legs outward. Others lay on the ground and rolled with laughter. I imagined I'd die of shame. My breathing came in short, hurried gasps.

Boys shouted, 'Catch me if you can,' and ran off. My heart quivered with pain and suppressed sobs. I swallowed the hard lump in my throat and clenched my teeth.

School was a nightmare. The iron gates and high brick walls made me think of a prison. A single word, a mere inflection of the voice, was enough to hurt my sensitive nature. I became more introverted—seeking peace in the bush with its scattered gum trees and low undergrowth like heath—lonely and weird. The wilderness and unbreakable silence had rules too, but I obeyed them by instinct. I was never bitten by a snake and, like a homing pigeon, I returned home when hungry or thirsty.

Mum never missed me or asked where I had been.

One day during a lunch break at school, I sat alone beneath a tree, feeling sorry for myself and munching my lunch. After eating I stood up, not knowing that the school bully had been stalking me like a beast-of-prey. He sneaked up behind me and kicked my back with such force that I fell to my knees and gasped. The pain drove me crazy. Stifling my agony, I chased him. He stopped, and turned, and laughed. His laughter rang out over the school yard. His burly figure towered above me and a grin plastered his face. Perhaps he thought I'd never dare defend myself.

Furious, I longed to smash his sneering smile. To hear him scream with pain and see his features distort. I drew back my leg and kicked — the boots and heavy irons giving me greater force. His face changed from derision to surprise and then to terror. Crying out in pain, he collapsed on the grass, howling like a whipped dog.

Mine was the victory. I glanced down at him. Blood trickled from his shin. Flies hovered overhead, like sharks at the smell of gore, waiting to land. I turned away, knowing he'd now leave me at peace.

Gone was the pain in my back. Gone was his smirking smile. Gone was his towering torso. His howl lived in my memory long after.

The next day the school principal sent for Mum. His jaw jutted and he glared at us. 'Colin is an unruly child. We do not permit fighting among our students. The school cannot be disrupted simply because your son can't take a joke.'

For once, Mum remained speechless. Then she turned on her heel and stamped out of the office. I knew she was in a rage because she grabbed my arm before stomping off. Mum didn't mind saying harsh things to me at times, but she'd go mad if anyone else tried to harm me.

When Dad came home, Mum's voice rose as high as it possibly could while relating the incident to him. 'I'm taking him out of school,' she fumed.

Dad fisted his hand. 'Use your nouce. Do nowt. He needs schooling.' He looked down at me and ruffled my hair. 'You stick up for yourself.'

Dad never said much. Perhaps he was too tired after a heavy day's work, or maybe it was because Mum kept nattering and never gave him a chance to speak.

Not long after, Mum removed the plaster casts and bandaged my legs each night to keep them straight. I stopped wearing the irons and wore special shoes. They looked normal but were heavy. Eventually, I didn't even need them anymore. *What a relief!*

The summer we arrived in Portland, hot Mallee winds swept down upon the town. It left me gasping for breath like a fish stranded on the shore. The dust-laden wind stung my eyes and clogged my nose, ears and mouth. Weeds curled with the heat. The whole town shut down because it was too hot to work, so Dad returned from work, filled the bath and dumped me into a tub of cold water.

'In the Mallee, where the winds came from, the crows fly backwards to keep the dust out of their eyes. You can't fly, so you must stay in the water to get cool.' He turned on the fan in the kitchen and joined Mum for a cup of tea.

What a good idea to fly backwards, I thought, and for days after, I tried walking backwards to keep the dust from my eyes.

Night descended. Like a bird, it swooped down, spreading its wings and blotting out the sky. It remained hot for days.

The government offered Dad a few acres of Mallee scrub, under the Soldier Settlement Scheme but Dad didn't take up the offer.

'The Mallee won't support a black snake,' Dad said. 'The Mallee eucalyptus are multibranched from the ground up and the soil is poor.'

Some British ex-army men accepted the deal but heavy machinery had cleared the landscape, leaving the area treeless. Without windbreaks, strong winds swept over the area, eroding the soil. With no drought-resistant trees, and no flowers to feed the birds and insects that had formerly frequented the trees, the land proved inhospitable. The settlers tried to scratch a living for themselves but half of them walked off their properties when their dreams failed to materialise.

Later on, the government split up several acres of rich land around Hamilton and gave free grants of prime property to those who had served in the Australian army.

Dad banged the table with his fist. 'The good land is reserved for Australian army veterans. I served in the *British* army so I'm not eligible for the grant.'

Dad's mate would pick him up in his car in the mornings and drive him to work. My father loved to be independent. 'I'll get my own car one day and build a house for Mum and you too,' he said.

I rocked myself with joy. The thought of having our own home and car was more than I'd dreamed of. It would be great to be dropped off at school. I'd love to see the looks on the boys' faces when we rolled up at the school gates in the mornings!

Dad bought a dray and a Clydesdale called Dobbin and when Mum found a job at the hypodermic needle factory, she drove the cart to work. The road went through hills and dales. Dobbin worked hard, pulling us up the hilly areas, but he refused to go downhill. He flicked his heels and turned around to stare at her when britching. Mum coaxed him but he stomped, pawed the ground and swished his tail until blood drained from her face and she unhitched the wagon.

To avoid these delays, she would take the longer route through level land. Dobbin was one of the few who got the better of Mum.

We also had a Jersey cow named Daisy. Mum milked her and I carried in the pail of rich, creamy milk to the house, sometimes dipping my finger into the froth and licking the cream.

I loved the two farm animals, especially Dobbin, even though I stood no higher than his knee at the time.

Dad worked from dawn to dusk. Eventually, he saved up enough money to buy a car and put our Clydesdale up for sale. When the new owners came to take him away, I clung to Dobbin's legs and wouldn't let him go. Dad unlaced my fingers one by one and Mum bore me off, kicking and crying.

The pain in my heart remained for a long time. I still cherish Dobbin's photo and to this day, I have a soft spot for all Clydesdales.

Dad drove the car to work, so after Dobbin's departure, Mum and I had to rely on a bus to go places. On our way to Hamilton one day, I became car-sick and a sour taste rose from my stomach.

I stamped my feet. 'Let me get off the bus.'

Mum tried to calm me but failed.

The driver thumped the dashboard. 'If you don't shut up and sit down quiet like, I'll stop the bus and belt you.'

I ceased stamping my foot, but only momentarily. 'I'm sick...' I began.

He braked so suddenly I nearly fell of my seat. Then he strode up to me and, like a colossus, he grabbed me by my arms, swung around, and put me down on the side of the road. 'What about it?'

I backed away from him in quick, jerky steps. I imagined myself spewing all over him and getting into even more trouble.

Through trembling lips, I cried, 'Amorryte. Lemme in.' In those days, I used Nottingham slang and strung my words together.

He jerked his head towards the bus and I scrambled in and sat with my arms draped around my knees, scarcely daring to breathe for the rest of the journey. My body shuddered with suppressed sobs. I no longer felt sick in the stomach. No longer felt like vomiting. I was cold. Cold with fear.

On our return home, Mum told Dad what had happened. I hid behind her and sneaked a look at him.

His smile fell upon me like a caress and broadened into a grin. 'Well, Old Reg Ansett was going to give you a hiding, was he? Good for him.' Dad had a kind heart, but that was his way of toughening me up to meet life's blows.

Reg Ansett owned a fleet of taxis up-country and had a network of routes connecting all the main towns. In later years, when he owned a fleet of planes known as Ansett Airlines, I often wondered how he treated the pilots who worked for him. *Was he as unkind to them as he'd been with me?*

Not all bus drivers were as impatient as Reg Ansett. I remember the old days when on my way to school in an old Bedford bus, we used to drive past a pear tree. One autumn day, the tree was laden with ripe fruit.

'Stop,' I cried. 'Please stop and let us pick pears.'

The driver drove off the road and parked his bus beneath the tree. 'Get on the roof to reach them,' he said. He helped us up before sitting back and lighting a cigarette.

We clambered up and filled our pockets and school bags with pears. Their delicate aroma filled the air. The bus was quiet for the rest of the way to school except for the sound of munching jaws and licking lips. The juice trickled down my arms.

When Mum saw the state of my clothes that afternoon, she glared at me. 'What have you been up to?'

'I didn't do nowt,' I blubbered, hoping she'd overlook the stains on my shirt for once.

Anyway, the sweet juicy pears were worth the hiding I had from Mum.

Chapter 3

WHENEVER DAD WAS FREE on a Sunday, he took us for long drives. Sometimes, we went to Heywood, about fifteen miles from home. At other times, he drove as far as seventy miles, along corkscrew dirt roads to Mt Gambier.

The car often broke down. The sight of Mum sitting beside the road on lonely stretches of highway with Dad bent over, fixing a broken clutch or a boiling radiator, remains etched in my memory. *How something so expensive leave us stranded in a desert of wilderness?*

Once we were back home, Dad would do most of the major repairs with the help of his neighbour, Cookie, who was a mechanic. I clearly recall our first car. Dad and Cookie replaced the canvas hood with a plywood cabin and turned the sedan into a utility. They laboured over it, pulling the old bomb to pieces, replacing and repairing worn-out parts. Dad spent so much time in the garage; I think it was his piece of heaven just as the bush and the sea were mine.

Dad eventually bought another car and left the old one in the yard as spare parts until it turned rusty and useless.

We always took a break at Hamilton, a distance of fifty miles from Portland. Mum would let me wander off while she and Dad lingered over their tea and scones.

Hamilton had a botanical garden with mature trees that shaded an expanse of lawns, where kangaroos hopped over and ate from our hands. Wombats burrowed in tree trunks, possums slept in cradles of ferns, and rabbits frolicked about. The garden also held some emus and caged parrots. One of the cages contained a lone monkey with brown eyes. Its antics fascinated me so much that I would climb trees and swing on the branches.

After morning tea, we drove to the next town and stopped at the fish co-op to buy mullet, cod or whiting. We would stop on the slopes of an extinct volcano, Tower Hill, where wild onions grew in profusion, and I'd help Mum gather them for pickling.

When peeling the onions, my eyes would prickle with tears, but I'd do anything to please my mother.

At the Victorian–South Australian border, Mum never failed to commemorate our crossing. She took photos of me standing with arms outstretched between the two white posts indicating Victoria on one side and South Australia on the other. Mum's enthusiasm, on these occasions, never ceased to fill me with excitement.

The Blue Lakes and sink holes of Mt Gambier were a poet's paradise. The lakes lay in the crater of an old volcano and turned from grey in winter to sapphire in summer. I'd stand gazing at the water, wondering what made them change colour. The town had many sinkholes and caves where feathery ferns clung to the sides, forming a lovely green lacework.

Nelson stands halfway between Portland and Adelaide. The name, Nelson, brought visions of the naval hero, Admiral Nelson, and a quivering sense of expectancy always rose within me as we approached the town. Solitude with its dusky wings reigned over the countryside. Massive gums dotted the islands in the waterway. The buildings stood on either side of a bitumen road. I clearly recall the corrugated roofs and low timber buildings, two shops, one pub and a garage—now known as a service station. The old frontier settlement served as a trading post for the farming community who lived along the peaceful Glenelg River.

'They rely on timber and fishing for their livelihood,' Dad said, and I knew from his tone that he'd love to live there too.

I dreamed of building a cabin for myself in this delightful haven. I didn't think of how I'd do it as I was too young to bother with such details. All I knew was that I wanted to enjoy nature. Whether it was the bush or the sea did not matter to me then.

Years later, when I lived in Canberra as a young man, I returned to Nelson during my holidays. To my surprise and delight, the surrounding area still filled me with the old familiar thrill of adventure.

The further from Portland we went, the more rugged the track became, until they were merely rough unsealed wagon trails, where large stones had been placed and smaller ones wedged between them to form a heavy-duty road structure. In other sections, broken stone served as a foundation and logs replaced them in the worst places.

Our car rattled and bumped over these corduroy roads, and my parents' teeth clicked in time to each rebound.

Mum held her handkerchief to her mouth. 'People only live here because they just can't stand the return journey.' Her voice sounded muffled.

During the mid-fifties, we often passed an aboriginal settlement that stood on the high side of a swamp. At times, a couple of Aborigines waited by the roadside.

Because Mum had received letters from England, warning us about 'the natives,' each time Dad drew near the aboriginal settlement, Mum would sing out, 'Keep your head down. Don't let them see you.'

That was the attitude of people in those days.

When we approached the burial site of a long-forgotten explorer who'd been killed by Aborigines during the last century, Mum's voice rose. 'There it is. He was speared by the blacks!'

Whenever we returned from Port Fairy and came to the mound with the white cross, Mum whispered, 'Always be on the alert. Never trust them.'

For weeks on end, I'd tremble with fear and my eyes would try to pierce the darkness for warriors lurking in the bush with spears uplifted.

My parents had come from the United Kingdom, where people had been brought up within a class system and everyone knew their place. Australia was spoken of as the colonies, and aborigines referred to as blacks. It was only when I met Johnnie, that I began to have an inkling of the word *prejudice*. Johnnie was the top shearer, and an Aboriginal who told us many dreamtime stories. Young as I was, I knew I could not tell my mother that I admired him.

My understanding of the class system inherent in my parents was reinforced when I visited England as a young man with my wife, Hazel. Mum's eldest brother, Clarence, had kindly driven us over to meet an aunt on my father's side.

We were about to leave when Aunt Ivy turned to my uncle and asked, 'If I see you on the street, may I speak to you?'

Shocked, I awaited his reply.

'You may,' he said, as if bestowing a privilege upon her!

It struck me then, that with such a rigid division of class structures, it was no wonder that prejudice was hard to eradicate.

When we'd first arrived in Australia, we'd stayed at the Smiths, who were Mum's distant relatives. Mum wrote to them frequently but we hadn't seen them for a long time.

One Sunday morning, at breakfast, Dad announced, 'It's time we visited the Smiths in Melbourne.'

Mum made sandwiches for lunch and we set off, my heart exploding with joy at the thought of seeing Grandpop and Grandma again.

On our way back to Portland that night, our car broke down near the explorer's grave. Mum went berserk and wouldn't allow Dad to get out of the vehicle or go for help. She grew hysterical and started at the slightest sound each time he broached the subject.

I shivered with cold, but she grabbed Dad's arm when he attempted to get a blanket from the back seat. She hung onto him, her face white. 'They may come and spear us.'

He struck the dashboard with his fist. 'It may be days before anyone drives by.'

I thought his thump was a crash of lightning and I shook with fear. Dad remained in the front seat and scanned the road. He hardly ever slept at nights. I think he suffered from insomnia.

Mum told me to climb over the seat and drag a blanket from the back. My eyes flicked from shadow to shadow, searching for an upraised arm holding a spear.

After a while, I shut my eyes. Hours passed. My stomach rumbled and grumbled enough to wake her. Faint with hunger, I pulled the sleeve of Mum's dress. 'I'm hungry. Anything to eat?'

'Have a piece of raw fish from the esky,' Dad said. He'd calmed down by then and his voice sounded soothing to my nerves, but the thought of chewing uncooked fish—bones and all, made me retch.

Mum handed me a bottle. 'Here's some water. It'll stop your stomach from rumbling.'

Dad rifled his pockets. 'No fags. Can't even smoke.' He flung his empty cigarette packet at Mum. Perhaps he hoped Mum had a packet in her handbag.

She caught it just like a cricketeer catches a ball, and turned to me. 'Stop blubbering and go to sleep. Someone is sure to come along soon.'

I imagined waiting in the car for days and dying of starvation. *The babes in the wood were luckier than me. The birds covered them with leaves and fed them. I have a blanket but no food.*

I shivered and drew closer to my mother. 'I'm cold, Mum.'

She took no notice. Perhaps she'd fallen asleep.

Worn out, I eventually drifted off.

Towards daybreak, the headlights of a vehicle broke the wall of darkness around us. Dad jumped out, flashed his torch and waved the motorist down.

The driver jammed on his brakes and stopped in a cloud of dust. He stuck his head out of the window. 'In trouble, mate?' His face was wrinkled and burned from the sun, but his eyes twinkled in the torchlight.

My heart swelled with joy.

Mum had joined Dad by now. 'We've broken down. Please help us.'

'Hop into your car. I'll tow you to a petrol station. It's not far off.' He got out and secured a short piece of rope to the front of our wreck. He then stepped on the accelerator and gradually took up the slack. Plumes of dust barrelled behind us. A rank smell arose from the exhaust pipe as the utility rumbled over the highway and stopped at the garage.

I loved country folk. They helped us when we were stranded and gave us tea and lots of advice.

Within two years of moving to Portland, Dad paid fifty pounds for a block of land on Learmonth Street. He drew up a plan of the house, took it in to the Council office for approval and commenced construction on our first home. In the evenings and on weekends, he built a kitchen, a workshop and a garage. He also made a shed that we used as a bathroom-cum-laundry and storeroom.

The Council condemned the structure, so Dad built two bedrooms and fixed things just enough to comply with their demands. His ingenuity was unsurpassable. Dad bought all the cast-off bricks from the old Portland hospital and constructed a wood burner from a metal forty-four-gallon drum to heat our water. Then he packed it with sand to hold the heat. He also laid a brick path between the kitchen and the bedrooms.

When the path was completed, Dad stacked the rest of the bricks in the backyard. Soon, rats and snakes infested the stacks. Mum screamed whenever she saw one, and became hysterical, so Dad carted them off on his trailer. He slaved half a day to clear the bricks and made several trips to the tip.

I tried to help him but Mum shouted, 'Come in. You'll be bitten by a snake.'

We moved into our home sometime in November 1951 when I was nearly six. Around this time, the butter ration, which had continued since World War 2, came to an end. Mum rejoiced because she loved baking cakes. That Christmas she spent the whole morning slaving over a wood fire. Sweat streamed down her face, and she wiped it with her apron. It left a dark streak on her cheek.

I pointed to the dirt, but she said, 'Wottjowant? I'm busy.'

Mum seldom strung her words together like I did, but she must have been thinking of the folk at home and lapsed into the Nottingham way of speaking. She sent me off to play, and rang a little bell when the meal was ready. I still recall the tantalising smell of hot roast and the colourful display of Christmas crackers on our white tablecloth. I smacked my lips after the main course, and drooled over the plum pudding.

Mum patted the tablecloth and smiled with satisfaction and pride. 'Just like old times.'

Dad wiped the sweat from his brow and slumped into his seat. 'Too hot to eat.'

'Wish we were back Home with the rest of the family.' Mum smoothed the spotless tablecloth and looked at Dad.

He shook his head. 'I'll never go back!'

Mum bit her lip. Young as I was, my heart crumpled to see her disappointment. She'd worked the whole morning to prepare this delicious meal and Dad hardly ate a morsel.

Chapter 4

OUR BLOCK OF LAND HAD been carved out of Joe Ward's farm. Old Ward and his wife lived about five doors down from us. An overgrown garden surrounded the house. Only a couple of sheep, a milking Jersey cow, and a brown and white billygoat now remained. The goat caused endless problems, chewing the rope that tethered him, and wreaking havoc in gardens. Even clothes drying on a line were not safe.

Once, on my way to school, I'd stopped to admire the goat's huge horns. Its pointed goatee reminded me of French artists I'd seen in my encyclopaedia. I approached, arm extended, to pat him. He lowered his head, pawed the ground and snorted like a bull. Then, kicking up the dust, he charged. To my young eyes, he appeared like a dragon breathing fire and smoke. I took off, not stopping until I reached the school gates, where I glanced back.

He stood on his hind legs with his forelegs on a neighbouring fence, tearing apples off the overhanging branches. How harmless he looked!

When Mum heard of the incident, she said, 'Don't be silly! He's only a billygoat.'

A few days later, the goat wandered into our yard and devoured the clothes on our clothes-line. Mum tried to chase him off with a broom, but the brute butted her, knocking her sideways. She soon sported a big purple bruise on her thigh from the encounter.

Ever since the goat had made a meal of his shirts Dad always made sure he shut the gate behind him when he left for work. In spite of that, Mum still never dared to leave the clothes on the line and she draped the half-dried shirts and dresses over our furniture. Headless spectres, their boneless arms waved in the breeze that wafted in through the open windows.

One evening, when Dad was working a night shift, I was playing on the back stairs in the fading sunlight. The ghost gums threw a dabbled shade, their shadows long; the tips of their branches like menacing fingers.

Mum's voice broke the silence. 'Colin, come inside. Old Ward's billygoat is here again.'

Her shrill warning sounded like a siren in my ears.

I raced indoors. 'Where is it?'

Mum stood in the front room, her eyes riveted to the front door. She wore a faded blue dress. Her blonde hair hung loose and caught the last rays of the sun. I rushed forward, but she barred the way. I dragged a chair to the nearest window, scrambled up and looked out. The goat was chewing Mum's prized peonies.

After demolishing the flowers, it tackled a post and gnawed away until the mailbox was left hanging at an alarming angle. Darkness fell. I switched on the outdoor light and dragged my chair to the bay window. The billygoat had nestled down on the doorstep. It twitched its stumpy tail, looking calm and placid.

'How did it get in?' Mum asked. 'Did you shut the gate when Dad went to work this morning?'

'Of course, I did.' *How could I forget to secure the place so soon after his attack on us?*

A stench slithered across and grabbed the back of my nostrils like an unemptied chamber pot. 'Worra pong. How do we get rid of him, Mum?'

'Don't worry, I'll soon fix him. In future old Ward will have to keep it tethered.' She left the room and returned, carrying a broom. Weapon in hand, she advanced and kicked open the door.

I braced myself, ready to shut it behind her if she rushed back inside. With thick twisted horns curling like gnarled tree roots, the goat dropped its head and charged. I held my breath until my lungs were about to explode. She leapt backwards, slamming the door shut behind her. I exhaled, thinking the worst was over.

Striding to the linen cupboard, Mum grabbed the methylated spirits. 'I'm not going to be beaten by a silly old goat.' Her eyes blazed. She held the bottle in one hand and groped in the cupboard with the other.

'Dad said you canna drink that without orange juice,' I piped up. I knew Mum was a teetotaller, and was only joking with her, but her expression scared me, so I scoured my brains for something to divert her attention from me. 'He's still here. He's still here.'

Electrified into action, Mum soaked an old dress with the spirits and moved towards the front entrance. I opened the door just wide enough for her to step onto the porch. She struck a match, turning the frock into an inferno. Inch by inch she advanced, waving the burning material at the beast. Amazed, I stood rooted to the spot. The billygoat nosed the flames cautiously. Its tongue shot out. Volleys of drool erupted from its mouth like a fire extinguisher. Enfolding its tongue around the flaming fabric, it swallowed flames and all, then shook its head. I stood in silence, terrified the goat would charge despite its singed whiskers and still-smouldering beard. *Will its insides be cooked? Will it spew out a stew of tripe?*

Mum backed away from the goat, and, electrified into action, I once again slammed the door shut. My mouth hung open.

Mum leaned against the door, breathing heavily. She stretched out her hand and snapped my mouth shut. 'Are you catching flies?'

How can she worry about my mouth at a time like this? My lips quivered. *What will happen to our veggie patch?* I imagined them trampled underfoot. Cucumbers squashed. Beans crushed.

Mum turned pale. 'I'll wait for your dad to return from the docks in the morning, but I'll stay up in case it manages to break in. You go to bed!'

It was long past bedtime. Too weary to remain awake, I curled up on the floor near Mum and dozed off.

Early next morning, the roar of Dad's car awoke me. My heart thudded. I rushed to the window, mounted the chair and pointed at the monster. Dad stuck his head out of the car window. He must have seen the goat because he nodded, backed the car out and drove down the laneway to the rear of the house. I raced to the back window.

Dad strode to the tool shed and returned with a pickaxe. 'Remain indoors.'

He waved his axe like a gladiator in the arena and marched up to the brute, gripping his weapon. The beast turned to face the enemy. I bit my lip and clutched the back of my chair. *Will the goat charge and gore my father to death?* My mouth grew dry. I slid the tip of my tongue over my lips.

Dad let fly with the axe handle on the billy goat's head. It stood still, not blinking a singed eyelid, its blackened beard pointing accusingly at him. Dad kept hitting and hitting. Perspiration oozed from his pores and trickled down, drenching his shirt even though the sun had barely risen.

Finally, he gave up. 'Going to get old Ward,' he shouted, and marched off.

I sneaked out from the backdoor and followed at a respectable distance. He kicked the door of Ward's house and entered, axe in hand.

After a few minutes, he came out with Farmer Ward and strode down the street. I followed. The farmer attached a heavy metal chain to the now-placid goat's neck. He pulled and Dad shoved until they succeeded in dragging it back to the farm.

After the farmer tethered the animal to a steel post with a short length of chain, Dad staggered home. His shirt was plastered to his back with sweat. I trailed behind, hoping he wouldn't turn around and see that I hadn't remained indoors. I imagined Dad's anger. Anger and belting. Belting that stung for days.

Once back home, Dad wiped his face with his already-sodden handkerchief. 'I'm knackered.'

I guessed he'd seen me but was too occupied with the goat.

Dad sank into his chair and ate his breakfast in silence. A vein in his neck throbbed in time to his chewing. Then he pushed his chair back.

'Old Ward has to borrow a .303 from Johnston. That should do the job. He's gonna shoot the bloody thing this arvo. About time it's put down.'

By late afternoon, the whole town knew that the old billygoat was to face the firing squad. Soon all Portland had gathered at Ward's place—grannies with their knitting and mothers with babies. I perched myself on the edge of the gutter and held my head high with pride in my dad.

Old Ward came out with the rifle and everyone went dead quiet as if the whole town held their breath and stopped their hearts. He chased the goat until it wound itself around the post. Helpless but defiant, it shook its head, then lowered it, threatening to butt him.

No one said a word while Old Ward loaded his gun and fired.

A deafening crack shattered the silence. A puff of smoke arose. The bullet hit its mark but the massive brute only shook its head as though chasing off a fly.

Once again, Ward aimed and fired. The billy goat raised its head defiantly, his goatee pointing at Ward, reminding me of D'Artagnan from *The Three Musketeers*, pointing his sword at his opponent.

The old billy goat took seven shots to the head before collapsing. Kicking its legs in a final attempt to fight off the enemy, it remained defiant to the last.

The men dug a pit and heaved the carcass in.

When Dad got home, he flopped down into a chair and fanned his face with his hat. 'Damn. Damn. Damn,' he said.

I'd never heard him swear.

The goat's presence lingered on. Everyone talked about the execution, and for months the front porch smelt like a piss-pot.

'The old goat caused more havoc than the Nazis did during the Blitz,' Mum said.

I'll never forget the billygoat defying all logic by eating the flaming cloth and resisting six shots to his head. It gave me a thrill and brought a sense of adventure to the routine of country life.

The excitement over the billy goat was soon eclipsed by a recession. When the economy of Portland sailed into headwinds, Dad was sometimes off work at weekends. Then people from the UK drew together, talking for long hours over the Old Country. Those reminiscent get-togethers were wings bearing them back to times that could never return.

I learned about Mum and Dad by listening to the adults rambling on, and from fragments of conversation between them. Dad had been born in Main Street, Carlton, Nottingham. Although a God-fearing man like his father, Dad never went to church except at christenings, weddings, or funerals.

My parents rarely attended church services, but Mum sent me to Sunday school. I enjoyed the Bible stories and the sing-alongs. Dad hated going to church. He told me that as a kid, he'd steal out to join his friends in a game of football instead of attending Bible study. At the end of the year, the chaplain presented a book to each child for his attendance at Sunday school.

'Well,' Dad said, 'when I came home without one, Mum asked, "Where's your Bible?" I put my hands in my pocket. "Didn't get one because I never turned up for classes." Mum's face turned as black as my old man's when he returned home straight from the coal pits. She half-flayed me alive.'

He shrugged his shoulders. 'She meant to teach me a lesson, but it only reinforced my belief that church-going people were hypocrites.'

Dad believed that religion had nothing to do with being good or bad, but despite his convictions, he let me make up my own mind about my beliefs.

'My family came from Manchester,' Mum said. 'My mother was strict. She prayed a lot but had a terrible temper.' She tossed her hair and her eyes sparkled. 'I have good connections. A distant relative, who lives in the Lakes District, owns the Lakeland Pencil manufacturing business and was knighted by the king.'

Mum reminisced with a far-away look in her eyes. 'Robbie, a cousin of mine, was a farmer from the West Country and was known as a highwayman.'

Intrigued by my ancestors, I asked, 'Was he was hanged?'

'No, he never broke the law, but neighbours called him a robber.'

'Like Robin Hood?' Tales of Robin Hood and his Merry Men always aroused my interest.

'Not generous like him. Because the main road passed through their land, the old man and his boys would bail up the stagecoach, demanding payment for the right of passage.'

Who'd dare refuse the Wild West gun-toting fellows, I wondered.

My maternal grandfather was a guard in the railways and we had lived in quarters near the railway complex until we left for Australia. Mum often spoke of his dedication to duty and of the pocket-watch that kept perfect time.

'Whenever a train passed the house he'd say, "That's the 9.50 to Sheffield, or the 2.51 to so-and-so." One day on his way home from Church, he keeled over and died.'

When we returned to England years later, my uncle and I went to visit grandfather's grave. His daughter, June, who is interested in family history, had a memorial stone erected for him.

My life was yet to unfold, and I was to face disappointment after disappointment before I visited the country of my birth and understood more of my origins.

Chapter 5

OUR HOME WAS ONLY a short walk from the coast. In the evenings, I would draw back the curtains and look out of the window before nestling down to sleep. A rocky cliff towered above the end of the street, and on clear nights, moonbeams danced on the water to the sound of the waves. At times, the moon glazed the quiet sea with a silvery light. Everything was peaceful, but when attacked by a storm, the ocean boiled in turmoil. Fascinated, I would watch a rip cutting through lines of breaking waves near the shore and making its way out to the sea.

On cold winter days, I used to wander on the shore, soak up the warmth from the sun and lick off the salt spray from my lips. At low tide, I'd watch the waves crash and splash on the rocks and search for shells or rescue fish and baby turtles trapped in little fissures. Everything about the briny ocean to the feel of gritty sand beneath my feet, held me captive.

Our house lay on the outskirts of the residential development of Portland, where untamed bush stretched for miles. It was about a mile distant from the abattoirs. Hidden by trees and scrub, workers slaughtered cattle, sheep and pigs and prepared the meat for packaging.

The bones were ground, then mixed with their blood and used as fertilisers. When the waste matter was pumped into the ocean, a brown patch appeared and grew in size like a genie menacing us with its pollution. The scum covered most of the bay area and attracted stingrays and sharks such as the grey nurse and white pointer.

The stink from the meatworks drifted towards the house whenever the boilers were opened. Mum and I smelled them, but Dad couldn't detect any odour.

I held my fingers to my nose. 'Why doesn't Dad get the stench?'

'He lost his sense of smell at the Belsen Concentration Camp.'

'Dad has never told me anything about the war.'

Mum's voice rose. 'That's because he tries to forget those terrible times.'

I slunk away, not wishing to anger her by asking any more questions.

One particularly stinking hot day, I found my father working on his car. His hands were black with grease and a can of Guinness stood by his side. I knew that Dad was usually in a good mood whenever he had a glass of beer, so I picked up the courage to question him.

'Why can't you smell anything, Dad?'

He gazed at me for a long time before speaking and appeared to melt away into the past. Looking back now, I realise that the rusty cogs of his mind, oiled by my words, were starting to move.

He rarely spoke of his experiences, but this time, he unburdened himself and let slip some of the horrors of war. His words poured out. 'On 15 April 1945, my regiment under Brigadier Glyn Hughes, advanced towards the Belsen Concentration Camp. We didn't know it at the time, but twenty-four hours earlier, the Germans had marched five hundred Jews from Auschwitz to Belsen, locked them in a barn and used a flamethrower on the wooden building.

'From miles off, the smell reminded me of decomposing cattle after a drought. The stench got worse as we approached the camp. Piles of dead lay around, filling the grounds right up to the front gate. Thousands of barely-alive prisoners lay huddled together in their own shit, on rotten straw. Typhus-bearing lice gnawed through their skin, exposing raw flesh.

'The stench was terrible. I lost my sense of smell from then. We picked our way through naked corpses to get to a group of living skeletons who stood around empty troughs. When we filled the troughs with water, they plunged their faces in and drank their fill. We knew they were starving, so we gave them our chocolate rations, but it made them sick and many died soon afterwards.'

I remained transfixed by his words. My legs turned to butter. My stomach churned.

Dad seemed to have forgotten me. He fisted his hands as though he was back again in Belsen. 'Infuriated with the Nazis, our Commanding Officer ordered Joseph Karmer, the Beast of Belsen, to load the dead onto trucks.' He dropped his head into both his hands. 'Tanks pushed piles of dead into pits and covered them with soil. Too many to bury by hand.'

I listened, not daring to interrupt in case Dad bottled up his feelings once more.

'At the beginning of hostilities, we did it for king and country, not knowing what we were getting into,' he said. 'Now, we don't talk about these things. We just want to forget.'

'Whatever happened to the Nazi Officer?' I asked.

'In 1945, Karmer was convicted of mass atrocities and sentenced to hang.'

Dad lapsed into silence and lit a cigarette. 'Before we left the camp, I discovered several crates of soap and posted out some out to Mum. It was a luxury in those days.'

Dad looked at me as if he was suddenly aware of my presence. 'Later on, I heard that the soap was made from human fat!'

'It had a good lather and brought your nappies fluffy and white,' Mum said, when speaking to me of the war a decade later.

Would Mum have used it if she'd known the truth, I wondered. In some countries, starving men ate the corpses of their mates. Hunger and necessity make people do things they normally wouldn't ever dream of. I hated the mere thought of war and yearned for peace. Peace within my family. Peace within the community. Peace in the whole world.

Portland had a natural deep harbour big enough for the fishing fleet that docked at a timber pier stretching out about a mile into deep-water. Due to the exposed nature of the wharf, loading and unloading cargo depended on weather conditions, so the City Council constructed a new breakwater at Portland. Currents then changed their course and the sea commenced to erode adjacent farms and homes.

A shiver of sympathy swept through me at the sight of houses crumbling and crashing into the raging waters. But what affected me most was that the water turned murky and the sand changed from glittering gold to a dull grey.

People then abandoned the teahouse, kiosk and shower rooms on the most beautiful swimming beach in Portland and went to Dutton Beach, which stretched for about fifty miles. It was part of a flat sandy plain built up over the years, and fossil hunters scoured the sand.

We had no lifeguards and tended to swim in groups for safety. The pier formed a cove where we played in the tranquil water.

I'll never forget the time someone yelled out, 'Shark! Shark!'

We stumbled out of the water. A red swirl appeared where we'd been a minute ago. In frenzy, women screamed, flew to their children and dragged them to the shore. Then they stood rooted to the spot like stone statues, clutching their dear ones.

A man tore up and down the foreshore, shouting, 'My son! My son! Anyone seen him?'

I recognised him. His son had been in the shallow water, while I'd been swimming further out among the breakers. *What if the shark had taken me instead? Why did it pass me and go to the little boy?* My lip trembled and I grew cold, thinking of my brush with death.

After the initial shock, people went out in boats, searching the water for signs of the child's body; others scoured the beaches in the hope of finding something. I joined the searchers, Prodding and pushing among bushes and reeds, looking for some sign of the boy.

The next morning while beach combing, I shooed away a flock of squabbling gulls and ran over to check what they'd been fighting over. A foul odour arose. A tangle of seaweed and sand exposed a bloody and mangled arm. I collapsed on the grass, gasping for breath. Nausea threatened to spin me round like a top. A tight sensation rose from my guts to my chest. I retched and retched and retched.

Soon, a swarm of flies swooped down.

When I recovered from the shock, I raced home and gasped out my story to Dad. I don't know what happened after that because Mum refused to let me show him where I'd seen the arm. I explained where it was, and Dad informed the police about the discovery.

The following day they buried the boy's remains. Nearly the whole town attended the funeral. Mum grasped my hand and my heart beat so loud, I wondered if it was about to burst. *If the shark had taken me instead, this would have been my funeral!* The incident is etched in my mind and every time there's a shark attack, I see the torn and swollen arm and get the stench of death.

'You're not to swim in the ocean unless we're with you,' Dad said. 'Find yourself a safe spot in a stream.'

Not far inland from the coast, my friends and I discovered a murky creek behind a row of sand dunes that flowed into the sea. I would swim or float on my back in about two feet of water and gaze at the clouds sailing across the blue sky, imagining I was back in the sea, hearing the screams of gulls and the roar of the ocean.

One day, gentle ripples broke the surface of the creek and beneath me I glimpsed a shadow. Sabre-sharp teeth brushed against my hand. I sensed movement along my arm, leapt out and raced for safety— feet barely touching the ground. My heart thudded and my teeth chattered. The air turned oppressive. The hair on my neck bristled.

My friends followed. No shark appeared. No flash of teeth. No fin or ripple.

It may have only been seaweed floating around with bits of shell embedded in it but the sea was never the same again. For a long time afterwards, I avoided going for a swim unless the floor of the sea was visible.

The Botanical Garden was another favourite haunt of mine. I listened to the trees creaking in the wind, and the birds calling and fluttering their wings. At the entrance, an iron roof kept the weather off one of the oldest lifeboats in the world—the *Portland*. I would often play around the frail timber boat with its scorched and scarred sides. Inspired by Herman Melville's *Moby Dick*, I imagined myself as Ahab in search of the doomed white whale. In my boyish mind, I tasted the salt on my lips and wiped the perspiration from my brow. The peeling paintwork turned into barnacles on a whaleboat and I rowed my boat, scanning the ocean till my eyes ached. The sun burned my skin.

The lifeboat was my companion for a large part of my early years, although at the time I remained in ignorance of its history. Built about 1885, the *Portland* gained fame because men had used it to rescue the shipwrecked *Admella*. The windjammer had struck Carpenters Reef on a voyage from Adelaide to Melbourne. Some sailors had lashed themselves to the rigging; others slipped into the boiling surf to their watery graves. The wreck of the *Admella* with the loss of eighty-nine lives is one of the worst disasters in Australian maritime history.

Nineteen people were saved by the men on the lifeboat, *Portland*. It is now proudly displayed in Portland's Maritime Museum.

At weekends, Mum and Dad sometimes visited their friend Maisie and her son Peter, who lived eighty miles from Portland, at Warrnambool. She had lost her husband over the English Channel when he'd flown a Spitfire during the Battle of Britain.

'He's due to arrive home from the war any day now,' she'd say, whenever we called on her.

Maisie's watching and waiting never faltered, and Mum and Dad couldn't bear to disillusion her.

Peter, an enthusiastic Ham operator, was much older than I was. I loved the visits to Warrnambool, and would slip away to join him in his room. I'd stand spellbound, listening to the distorted voices rising and falling from some far-off place on the ham radio. Snatches of conversation rose to the surface like bubbles in a pond. The voice sounded eerie, fading in and out until loss of contact. *How uncanny to hear people speak of personal things to strangers!*

Over the years, the tie between us weakened and we passed one another like ships in the sea. I missed listening to voices from distant lands, never realising that, within a few years, we'd be watching people from faraway as they spoke on television.

Time passed. Lucerne ripened, was harvested and packed into bales for winter fodder. Milk poured into factories and was churned to butter for export. In spite of all that industry in Portland, bills and living expenses consumed our entire earnings. Building jobs at Portland became scarce.

Since Dad wasn't eligible to get a grant for good land, he decided to work for landowners where the land was fertile. He was never afraid to have a go at anything.

I thought of it as an adventure, but Mum foresaw nothing but disaster.

Chapter 6

TO THIS DAY, THOUGH I no longer live in the bush, its influence is still with me. Perhaps it came from my nomadic childhood when we moved from one small town to another— so alike, at times I couldn't tell them apart. Each had a general shop, a produce store and a pub.

At one such town, a woolgrower gave us a tin shed to live in and provided us with meat and vegetables in return for Dad doing a building job. Our home had a dirt floor and corrugated iron sheets on three sides with hessian hanging over the open side to keep out the cold. Dad nailed some more to the rafters to serve as partitions for our bedrooms but Mum complained of the stuffy little room. She complained of the smells. She complained of the heat.

Dad shrugged. 'At least we have a roof over our heads and free meat and vegetables. We won't starve.'

I attended classes for a term in the local bush school, but we kept relocating whenever Dad completed a job, so I had to study by correspondence.

Dad made sure I learned the work prior to filling in the worksheets. 'Otherwise, when you grow up, you'll be digging ditches or cleaning latrines.' His words left me with a thirst for knowledge that increased as the years passed. Enthusiastic over the homework, whenever I needed help and Dad was busy working, I turned to Mum.

'Just copy the answers out of the book. What do I care?' she said, without raising her eyes from her knitting.

Mum checked that all the questions were answered and, regardless of whether they were correct or not, she posted the papers back to the Education Department.

My studies were as colourful as her patchwork quilt, but didn't look as good.

When Dad saw my marks, he fumed and took a few paces towards Mum with clenched fists. 'You remain at home with nothing to do but cook, yet you couldn't check the boy's work.'

Mum flung a plate at him. 'I'm sick of living like this. When are you going to find some steady work?'

Dad sprang back and the plate smashed on the floor, sending little slivers of china to every corner of the room. He strode out of our shack and drove off in the car without his dinner. I guess he called in at the nearest pub.

I recall being grief-stricken at having been the cause of another argument between my parents. I slunk back to my room. My chest heaved. A sledge-hammer battered my ribs, bruising my heart and squeezing my lungs. The pain tore at my heart. But what could a six-year-old do?

Joe, who lived on a farm with his sister Jenny, worked for Dad as a labourer. 'Somewhere over there,' he said, jerking his head in a vague direction.

Country folk spoke of things being 'just down the road,' which could mean anything up to 20 miles. These expressions lingered in my mind, and I find myself using them even as an adult.

There were golden days and grey days. Jenny took me into Hamilton whenever she drove to town in their Model-T Ford. The former owners had tried to fix the rear door of the car years ago, but the hinges still shrieked in protest. When Jenny cranked, the motor shuddered for a few seconds before the vehicle snarled and snorted into action. The jalopy had no floor and the seats had gone. I sat on an old banana box Jenny had placed on the framework and put my feet up on the dashboard.

Hamilton was only fifteen miles away, but the trip took about an hour. The windshield had broken long ago, and the wind threw dust, leaves and twigs onto our faces. We chugged along, slowing down on hills or even on slight rises. Walking would have been quicker. The brakes didn't work, but Jenny seemed to know when to shut the engine. She would let the car roll to a stop until the groaning tyres came to rest against the kerb or a ditch. I'd hold my breath and wonder whether the car would stop or keep going until it crashed into a tree.

Despite all that, I loved those jaunts into town. Tree-ferns grew among the gaunt gums, and sunlight made chequered patterns through the leaves. Perched on the banana box, I enjoyed the scenery and especially adored the delicious cakes Jenny brought along for us.

One day, Dad and I visited a large property near Wannon Falls, outside Hamilton. A wide gravel road framed on either side by swathes of farmland stretched ahead of us. Weatherboard houses lined both sides of the road and flowerbeds gave a splash of colour to the green background. In the distance, the slate-grey roof and white walls of a manor on top of a hill stood out with its profusion of yellow chrysanthemums and multi-coloured pansies.

I longed to jump down and pick some for Mum, but Dad restrained me. 'That's Malcolm Fraser's house on top of the hill. You'll get a clip on the ear from the gardener if you lay a finger on them.'

Malcolm Fraser would enter Parliament a few years later. In 1975, when Sir John Kerr dismissed the Whitlam Government, Fraser, who was

Leader of the Opposition at the time, formed a Caretaker Government. He served as Prime Minister from November 1975 to March 1983. I never had the opportunity to meet him at Wannon Falls, but saw him several times when we moved to Canberra.

I remember the time Dad had to pick up a labourer who lived on a large property nearby. He pulled up outside the labourer's home and gave a little beep with his horn.

The property-owner strode over, placed his hands on his hips and looked us up and down. His forehead puckered up in a frown and his chin jutted. 'Don't drive the bloody car up here, mate. It wears out the road.'

He must have swallowed some of the gravel from the road, because his voice was harsh.

Dad's colour rose and a pulse near his throat throbbed. He put his foot down on the accelerator and drove off, throwing up clouds of dust behind us. Then he parked on the verge beside the public road.

From then on, the labourer had to walk all the way down the long track, so Dad could pick him up. Dad fumed over the loss of so much time. Fortunately, most of the big landowners didn't mind us using their private road.

Dad took me along whenever he went into town for a haircut. The sight of the red-and-white pole outside his shop gave my heart a lift. The barber was clean-shaven and tall. He dressed casually, with a T shirt and denim jeans. An impressive array of scissors and clippers and combs lay on a table. The barber also trimmed beards and carried out wet shaves with a sharp cut-throat razor. Best of all, he always told interesting yarns.

'Did you know old Farmer Jones never bothers to change his car tyres? He just abandons his car,' he said one day.

Dad laughed. 'You're joking!'

'No. Fair dinkum. Only yesterday, he came in to buy a new car. When the salesman asked if he wished to trade in his old one, he said he'd left it on the paddock as it had a flat tyre.'

'I'll take the car off his hands for nothing, mate,' Dad said. 'These cockies have too much money.'

The barber leaned forward and whispered, even though we were the only ones in his shop.

'His neighbour trades in his Mercedes as soon as his ashtray is filled. He has to keep up with the Jones.'

Dad's laughter bounced off the walls. I loved his infectious laugh, and joined in, although I couldn't see the joke. I believed the barber, as I'd seen farmers loading sick sheep in the boot of their Mercedes and driving off to the vet. *It seems a shame to soil their cars but why don't they use their ute instead?*

Dad built an extra fireplace for Farmer Jones. When he'd completed the mantelpiece, I ran my hands on the cool smooth surface of the ceramic tiles. I longed for a fireplace and imagined myself sprawled on a carpet, reading before a blazing fire during winter.

Just as Dad was packing his tools to leave, the landowner swaggered in, holding a magazine. He showed Dad an advertisement for a kitchen stove. 'My new stove has just arrived. Could you install it in the kitchen before you go? It's my wife's birthday present and must be in as soon as possible.'

Dad eyed the picture. 'This must have cost you half the price of your stock!'

'Life's short, and you're a long time dead, mate,' the farmer replied.

Wool had created a 'bunyip aristocracy' and the wealthy always had the best of everything. Each farmer tried to rival his neighbour, and wanted a bigger this, or a better that because Australia rode on the sheep's back at the time, and farmers held the reins.

In 1956, when television first went to air in Australia, the cockies had them installed in time to watch the Olympic Games. The women were excited because the Duke of Edinburgh was to open the Games in Melbourne.

We were keen to watch the events but could only dream about such luxuries.

After Dad completed work on Farmer Jones's property, we moved to Byaduk, a small settlement about 15 miles from Hamilton. We stayed rent-free in the farmer's old cottage in exchange for building a fireplace in the new homestead. I was delighted to live in a real house near a store that sold ice cream made from fresh cream. I'd sniff the ice cream, take a lick of the creamy, cold caramel, close my eyes and let the taste dissolve on my tongue. Its smooth texture remained for a long time. I licked and licked until there was nothing left.

We spent Easter at Byaduk, and Mum bought me an ice cream Easter egg. It remains one of the most treasured memories of my childhood.

In the early days, Dad used to buy his petrol in forty-four-gallon drums, which he tipped out into smaller containers that I held for him. When we'd poured the rest into the petrol tank of our car, it splashed on us. Our clothes stank and I choked from the fumes, as if someone had wrapped a blanket around my head to smother me.

Byaduk had a modern petrol bowser. Dad rocked a lever back and forth to fill a big glass container on top of the bowser. When filled, the petrol rose and flowed into the petrol tank of our car. We no longer had dry hands and stinking clothes.

What would scientists think of next?

One hot summer day, Dad took me to a creek known as the Stony Rises. Green algae covered most of the area in and around the natural swimming pool. Some sections were algae-free and the clear water revealed huge honeycombed-stones.

'This was a lava flow from a volcanic explosion,' Dad said. He stepped into the water and shuddered. 'The water is icy but it'll get the heat out of your body.'

I sat at the side and slid in, eager to cool off on such a hot day. The cold water gripped my ankles. Sharp spears of pain ripped through my body. My teeth chattered. I kept slipping on the slime and shivered—not only from the cold but from fear. My breathing came in short gasps. The water reached up to my neck, so I tried to climb out but fell back with a splash. *Will I swallow the slimy water and choke to death? Am I going to drown?*

Dad helped me out. He looked like a man from Mars. Green hair. Green body. Green limbs. A quivering mass of green.

'Perhaps the men from Mars were green because they are covered with moss because they live so far from the sun,' I stammered when I finally reached dry land.

Dad's grin grew bigger until his eyelids became mere slits. Then he burst out laughing. We couldn't stop chuckling until we arrived home.

Mum never saw the funny side of things. She put her hands on her hips and screamed. 'What have you been up to? Do you want to make the boy ill? I have enough on my hands without having to look after a sick child and washing dirty clothes.'

She grabbed my shirt collar, dragged me to an old horse trough, turned on the hot water tap and half-filled it. 'Now get in and soap yourself well. And don't forget to wipe behind your ears when you dry yourself.'

I never did appreciate Dad's ingenuity of constructing a hot-water tank with a tap as I did when the welcome warmth of the water thawed my freezing body.

Mum waited until my shivering stopped. Then she left to continue her quarrel with Dad.

We drifted off to Macarthur when farmers in the Byaduk area no longer needed Dad's services. The travelling picture-show man visited the place once a fortnight on a Saturday, and every man and his dog, from Jo's mongrel to the pampered pooch of the biggest landholder, went to the cinema at the Town Hall. We sat in un-numbered deck chairs—first-in best-dressed. The chatter of the projector drowned the voices of the actors, and cigarette smoke turned the screen into a sea of fog. Loose sheets from the corrugated-iron projection-room clattered overhead, but nobody complained.

After the show, one and all, big and small, yarned over their cups of tea and slices of cake. They spoke about various things but never discussed the film they'd just seen. The fostering of mateship at these functions seemed more important than anything else.

At times, entertainers like Slim Dusty or Chad Morgan performed at a concert. They swung lassoes and sang country-and-western songs. Years later when I moved to Brisbane, I saw them once again at the Tweed Heads Bowling Club. It revived memories of old days and I was filled with nostalgia.

Life in the bush laid its mark on me. Macarthur had its own barber, who told me to part my hair on the right side as I had a double crown. I still comb it that way—one of the lifelong habits I picked up in the countryside!

Later on, we shifted to Branxholme and lived in a rented caravan on a property next to the building site where Dad worked. He always took me along, and I'd watch farmers planting their crops or bringing in the harvest.

Sheep had a rough life. Farm hands forced them into deep, concrete trenches full of chemicals and pushed their heads under the water to remove ticks. Some of the ticks were as big as a three-penny-bit. Huge, ugly things. I imagined that, after being nearly drowned, the sheep dared not carry anymore vermin for fear of re-dipping, and my heart ached for them.

One day, hearing an ailing lamb bleating mournfully in the distance, we followed the sound. As we approached, an awful smell greeted me. Crows had pecked out the lamb's eyes and were tearing out its guts, which looked like a bowl of spaghetti and cheese smeared with tomato sauce. My stomach clenched at the sight of the bleeding eye sockets and torn insides. I swallowed the lump in my throat as the farmer raised his rifle and put the poor thing out of its misery. I knew then, why the expression 'Stone the crows' became popular in outback Australia. After that, even the sound of their cawing was enough for me to reach for the catapult in my belt.

I was always welcome at a farm, especially at harvest time. I guess it was because I helped gather the potatoes and pumpkins and pitched into any light work. I loved opening and shutting gates. It felt good to lend a hand and be appreciated.

When bringing the day-old lambs back to shelter, I would cuddle them and put my face to their silky new wool. A farmer gave me a lamb once. I hugged it to my chest all the way home.

As soon as I entered the house, Mum said, 'What have you brought home now?'

I held up my pet, hoping she'd coo over the dear thing. 'The farmer gave it to me, Mum. Isn't it cuddly?' I bent and nestled my head in the woolly bundle.

Mum put her hand upon my shoulder and shook me. 'Do you expect me to clean up its droppings? Take the filthy thing back tomorrow. Do you hear me?' She punctuated each sentence with a shake to emphasise her words.

I swallowed my sobs and raced to my room. *Why does Mum disapprove of everything I do?*

One day at a large property, the farmer whisked me off my feet and set me down on his tractor. He placed a cushion for me in the driver's seat, so I could reach the pedals, and taught me how to use the gears and brakes.

'Now you can sow the seeds,' he said.

Delighted, I grabbed the steering wheel and concentrated on driving in a straight line along the rows. They seemed a couple of miles long. I breathed in the smell of manure and the sun-warmed earth, and listened to the sound of grass being ripped up and chewed by the tractor.

Years later, I told my wife about driving a tractor from the age of seven. She was stunned.

'Most farm children do the same thing,' I said. 'In the country, everyone has to pitch in with the work.'

At shearing-time, the shearers competed with each other. Some nicked the sheep and took off a bit of skin in their haste. Then the sheep's wound would have to be smeared with tar and shorn sheep ran around, bleating in distress, with tarry black spots all over them. Johnnie, an Aborigine, was among the top shearers. He hardly ever made the sheep bleed.

When he had done his quota, he'd ask, 'Does anyone need a haircut?'

Everyone queued up to have their heads shorn for free, so I lined up with them too.

Johnnie used his sheep-shearing shears. I feared he'd nick me, but he did as good a job as the barber. He must have been inexhaustible because after a long day of shearing sheep and cutting hair, he told us his dreamtime stories. We children gathered around him, our faces brightening like light globes as we listened. My mouth hung open, believing every word.

My favourite tale was *Why Kangaroos have Black Paws*. Johnnie described a bush fire in such detail that fire hissed and crackled in my mind, as he spoke. He mimicked the sounds and actions of a kangaroo, stamped on imaginary flames with his hind feet and used his forefeet to extinguish the sparks. Finally, Johnnie hopped to a nearby stream and placed his paws in the water to cool them and wash off the soot.

'They remained black forever,' he said. 'That's why kangaroos have black paws.'

Johnnie was the only Aborigine I ever got to know as a child. If Mum had found out how close we were, I think she'd have had me fumigated. Such was the prejudice in those days!

My parents lived like gypsies. Once a fortnight, we returned to Portland for a couple of days to collect the mail. Highways had a thin ribbon of bitumen down the centre, but most roads were narrow and our Ford 10 was slow. One day, after returning to Branxholme, Dad realised he'd left some essential tools behind, so we drove back home to Portland. The trip took hours even though the town was only about thirty-five miles away. The boneshaker snorted like an elephant with influenza, and roared down steep hills on bitumen roads at fifty miles per hour. On dirt tracks, it chugged along at walking pace.

A few days later, the old wreck staggered out of the garage for the last time, and Dad bought another clunker.

Life in the bush was hard for Mum. Her friends back in Portland always had time for chatting over a cup of tea, but country women worked most of the day and had little time for idle gossip. Mum had no social life, and living like a gypsy brought on more mood swings.

Every so often she'd shout, 'Get out of my way and give me some peace.'

I'd set out for solitary rambles in the bush, absorbed in wonder at its quiet majesty. Sometimes, I'd lie down, pull my Akubra over my face and watch lizards lazing in the sun through the holes in my hat. I loved the frilly lizard and the blue-tongued one.

Most snakes shied off from humans and were clever conjurors at disappearing. I admired the beautiful grass snakes and wanted one as a pet.

Mum said, 'I never heard of such nonsense.'

The bush was my solace—my guardian. I never lost my way there, but at times, the longing for Portland with the seashore and cliffs grew intense. I missed the beautiful heath plants with their tall straight tuffs. I missed scrambling up the sandstone ridges golden with gorse, where thorny bushes gave way to the gums. I ached for the sea with a hungry longing.

Little did I realise, I'd soon be back at Portland.

Chapter 7

AFTER SEVERAL MONTHS OF WANDERING around in the Victorian bush, Dad finally gave in to Mum, and returned to Portland. I hopped on my toes in delight, thinking of the rocky cliffs, sandy shores and seashells.

Mum escorted me to school on my first day of Grade 2. Hundreds of feet kicked up the dust as we entered the grounds. Boys laughed and shouted, welcoming each other, but no one said, 'Hello,' to me. My enthusiasm plummeted.

In the classroom, the salty sea smell competed with the unfamiliar odour of newly sharpened pencils and books. The room was six rows deep with four double desks. I picked a seat in the last row as far away from the teacher as I could get. The day dragged on. The roar of the ocean from my classroom window kept calling me, and I looked towards the window, hoping to catch a glimpse of the sea.

My teacher rapped her cane on my desk. 'You're behind in your studies. I'm sending you for an interview with a Guidance Counsellor to have your reading and spelling skills tested.'

She clutched my hand, dragged me along and knocked at his door.

The counsellor was a Scot and a Scottish burr stuck in his throat. 'How many Rs are there in rabbit?' He pinned me with his eye and held me at rapier point.

I stood before him, shifting my weight from one foot to the other with my eyes fixed on a worn-out patch of carpet. 'Several,' I replied, thinking they were too many to count.

'Stupid boy!'

I jerked up my head. His face had turned as red as a beetroot. He grabbed my hand, led me down a corridor and placed me in a special class.

There I remained until my reading skills improved. My spellings continued to be atrocious but in arithmetic, I managed to figure out the answers to my sums. I've always been quick at working things out in my own way.

'How did you get these numbers?' the teacher said. 'You must have copied the work from another boy!'

His words made me lose the last vestiges of interest I had in my studies. I seldom spoke to other children. When spoken to, I replied after a brief pause. Most of the kids did not understand my Nottingham accent and slang anyway. My teacher tried to teach me what she called *correct* diction. However, I fell back into my native dialect, joining words together when excited or angry or frustrated. I kept apart from the others and my leaden lips refused to give voice to my thoughts. I'd shift in the chair and cross and re-cross my legs or slip my hands into my pockets.

I developed a pain in my jaw from grinding my teeth, so I skipped classes. I created my own world and wandered off to the beach or the bush, listening to the cries of whipbirds and butcherbirds, the hooting of owls and the shrieks of parrots. There, I occupied myself in a close communication with nature and exulted in the saturation of my senses.

Whenever the principal reported my absence to Mum, Dad thrashed me. 'So you spent the day fishing, did you?' he said. 'This will teach you not to do it again!'

His belting stung for days, but when the discomfort ceased, I was off. Only now, I'd wait until after roll call and then slip away unnoticed. *Why doesn't Dad realise that I learned nothing from school, anyway?*

School also sucked the life out of teachers. Sometimes, I overheard the older students say, 'Old so-and-so has hanged himself' or 'Miss Brown is in the loony bin.'

Once, a member of the staff left without saying a word and we wondered who'd teach us.

That afternoon, on my return from school, I stammered out to Mum, 'Teacher hasn't turned up. Do I need to go to school to-morrow?'

Mum only glared at me. The next morning, she stormed over to the principal. 'When will Colin get a new teacher?'

He shrugged his shoulders. 'Just wait and you'll know.'

I remember once, only a couple of hours before the final exam, our teacher walked up and down the room, sporting a ferocious frown. 'The questions posted out from Melbourne are not based on what I've taught you lot. Forget the year's work and do your best.' He left the room and disappeared.

On returning home, I said, 'Mum, we weren't taught anything that was in the exam. The teacher was so angry. He stomped out of the room and didn't come back.' I bit my bottom lip and hoped I'd be taken out of school, but nothing happened.

Soon after his departure, we had a new teacher. One day, Mum stroked my hair and looked deeply into my eyes. 'Did your teacher ever hug or kiss you?'

'No, but he often has his arm around his favourites and takes them for separate classes.' I shrugged my shoulders. 'Perhaps they need more help.'

Mum tousled my hair.

A few days later, I heard that some parents had prosecuted a member of the staff.

Around this time, my parents bought me ten volumes of the *Children's Encyclopaedia* by Arthur Mee. The encyclopaedia provided a refuge from isolation and hurt, and brought the arts, philosophy and history of the world to life. The author set problems and gave examples on how to work them out. The illustrations captivated me, and the books became my most prized possession. My inquiring mind wanted to delve further, and I spent hours learning amazing things and amassing knowledge.

I did not care for attention and never received any. Divine intervention must have smiled on me because, despite all the drawbacks, I achieved average results at the end of the school year.

My growing thirst for knowledge aroused an interest in other books too. I loved stories of Robin Hood and adventure stories like *Treasure Island*. The classroom bored me witless, but books opened up a window of life to me and I peered through with a wildly beating heart.

Reading got me out of Mum's hair. On rainy weekends, I curled up in bed, listening to full frog symphonies and losing myself in a book. I no longer was restless. I no longer tapped my foot on the floor. I no longer gazed at the door. I had my books to turn to.

Books were my companions on sunny weekends too. The beach was a favourite spot to read. I lay there on my stomach and let the sun warm my back. The sea breezes blew the pages and sand sometimes got into my eyes. Then I'd sit in silence, staring at the flow of the tide, watching ripples kiss the seashore. The beach was my hallowed place where I escaped from Mum's nagging.

At times, Mum grumbled, 'You're hardly ever at home to run errands for me or do the chores.'

Older and braver now, at seven, I took no notice.

I never forgot the hurt I suffered during the first months at school, when bullies surrounded me by day and haunted me at nights. School was a nightmare, so a wall of books served as a protective barrier between me and the rest of the boys. I read at playtime, oblivious of my surroundings. Warmth would spread throughout my body and a feeling of euphoria enveloped me when reading. I learned to view things from a different perspective and developed contempt for my fellow students, who only found pleasure in games.

Some kids called me 'a Pommy bastard'. I didn't know what it meant, but I knew it was intended to be an insult. I paid them back in my own subtle way and used sarcasm as a weapon. It is said that the pen is mightier than the sword. In my case, by the time I'd left school, my tongue was sharper than the sword and would cut anyone who taunted me.

Every week, I went to the Post Office to fetch the mail from relatives in England. One of Dad's work mates who was from Yugoslavia, often gave me his stamped envelope, so I started to gather stamps. My collection multiplied as the influx of people from Europe increased.

Three types of people now lived in Portland—the Australians, the British and the New Australians, whom the boys at school called *wogs*. Years later, I read that the term *wog* originated during the time the Suez Canal was under construction. The British government had issued Egyptian workers with uniforms. Stamped on the backs of their shirts was the word, WOGS. It stood for *working on Government Service*.

The British became shopkeepers. Italians and Greeks ran the milk bars or take-away fish-and-chip shops; the Dutch community controlled the bakeries. The smell of freshly baked bread, cakes and pies roused pangs of hunger whenever I passed the baker's shop, so I'd dash in and buy my favourite beef-and-mushroom pie.

My parents kept strong ties with friends and relatives back home, and every week, Mum's brother, Stan, and his wife Anne, posted out a copy of *The Nottinghamshire Guardian*. Dad and Mum devoured the papers and re-read them over and over again. Sometimes the mail contained little gifts for me. Dad's younger sister, Aunt Winnie, always sent me a card for my birthday and enclosed a small present—mainly sweets. When I grew older, the envelope contained a five-pound note. The money came in handy, especially as I was saving to buy a car.

My aunt continued this until my marriage in 1971. Then every year, she would either send an exquisitely woven tablecloth from the lace factory, or a doily of Nottingham lace. My wife and I loved the delicate handiwork. We framed and hung them in our lounge room. I particularly cherished the one entitled, 'No Place like Home.' It showed a room that had a ceiling with exposed beams. The chairs stood on either side of a fireplace with a cheerful fire.

Aunt Winnie had been bridesmaid at my parents' wedding. After their deaths, she corresponded regularly and revealed many things about Dad that had for years remained a closed book.

I remember once when she wrote saying, 'Your Dad had a soft spot for me. When he left school and commenced work every evening, he'd bring home a bag of sweets, a chocolate or a piece of cake for me. We were devoted to each other.'

I treasured her letters and, as an adult, I delved into my family history, eager to learn more of my roots. From Dad's side I descended from a long line of furniture makers. No wonder I've always enjoyed working with wood. Now that I've retired, I turn wooden bowls and boxes as well as beautifully crafted pens.

Mum's great-great-grandfather had worked as a gamekeeper for a lord and lived on his manor. He looked after the birds, beasts, trees and plants on the lord's estate. Perhaps that's why I love the bush and have a green thumb and grow orchids as a hobby.

Some of my ancestors were highwaymen. Another owned the Lakeland Pencil Factory in the Lake District. What a cross-section of people my forefathers were!

Whenever my parents visited friends, Mum would say, 'Little children should be seen and not heard.'

I'd sit on a chair, swing my legs up and down and listen to the chatter around me. From their conversations, I learned that friction often occurred between churches of different denominations. During one of these get-togethers, I heard an interesting story about an Anglican minister and a Roman Catholic priest. Both had served together as chaplains in the army and been good mates. When posted to Portland after the war, they renewed their friendship. Their respective churches, built from blue stone ballast brought out from England in immigrant ships, reflected their camaraderie. It was rock-solid.

Parishioners from the Church of England disapproved of their mateship and complained to their bishop. He sprang into action and transferred the minister to New Guinea.

I'll never forget the time when the congregation gathered to farewell him. He delved his hand into his pocket and took out a letter from his predecessor in New Guinea. Slowly, he unfolded it and read the contents:

Welcome to the heat, rain, mosquitoes, leeches and crocodiles. If one of them doesn't get you, the other will. His voice droned on, relating all the hardships he'd face. Women shifted in their seats and men tugged at their collars with red faces as if they were about to choke.

The letter must have given their conscience a twinge, because after the service they departed in silence with bowed heads.

An ache rose to my throat. I longed to tell the chaplain I was so sorry to see him go but bashfulness sealed my tongue to the roof of my mouth.

This shyness remained with me for years and continued until I reached my prime.

Chapter 8

DURING THE LONG SUMMER school holidays, Dad frequently drove us out west for about thirty miles to Swan Lake along the Glenelg River, where the water is clean and clear. So clear, you can see right to the bottom.

Our neighbours, Ian Cook and his wife Pat, together with their two sons, Robert and Barry, always accompanied us to Swan Lake. Dad would park beneath a large mulberry tree and we kids played in the shade of the huge horizontal branches. The men went fishing in the Glenelg River, while our mums picked mulberries.

Some time ago, Dad had seen a body floating in the lake and had to report the matter to the police. He knew it was tempting to dive down and swim among the marine life and vegetation below, when we walked on the wooden launching platform.

'Don't swim in the lake. People have been drowned there,' he warned us, before he left.

After wandering over to the lake and gazing into its fascinating depths, we returned to help our Mums pick berries. We ate as many as we placed in the buckets. It left our faces, hands and clothes stained a dark purple. For days after, the delicious aroma of crusty pastry drifted through our houses. Mulberry and apple pie with fresh cream was a heaven-sent luxury in those times, so our visits to Swan Lake are among some of my fondest memories.

At the time, the lake was only known to the locals, but now it is part of the Great South West Walk. The walk is a 250-kilometre loop that begins and ends at the Maritime Discovery and Visitor Information Centre in Portland, Victoria. It winds around three National Parks, the pristine Glenelg River, the picturesque town of Nelson, sand dunes, sandy bays and beaches and rugged cliffs. The circuit boasts of a diversity of flora and fauna.

Old Jenkins ran a dairy farm just up the road. Each morning, Mum handed me some cash to buy a half-gallon billycan of milk and a pint of cream.

The farmer would give me the cans filled to the brim and wink at me. 'Mind you don't spill any of it, lad.'

His wink was an invitation to taste the cream. I strode home with a spring in my step. The cream spilt and streamed down the can, so I'd stop and run my finger on the outside and lick it. As I tilted it to clean one side, the contents ran down the other. I swung the can, relishing the sweet flavour and soft texture over my tongue. The more I did this, the more cream oozed out.

At times, too excited to wipe the tell-take signs from my lips, I arrived home with a moustache of cream and handed Mum the pail. She would glance inside and give me a clip on the ear. I'd stagger back.

In later years, a milkman drove a horse and dray to our door and delivered milk and fresh cream in billycans we'd left at the doorstep, so I no longer had to run errands to Old Jenkins.

Time passed. The milkman substituted a van for his horse and cart, and carried the milk in glass bottles. Milk took on a bluish haze and never tasted the same.

Mum said, 'They've added water to the milk. Shake the bottles before opening them, so they'll look a bit more like they used to.'

I remember the shiny tinfoil tops on the bottles. If we didn't bring them in straight away, the magpies used to peck them to get at the cream on top. It was my job to bring in the milk bottles as soon as they arrived and I would listen for the sound of the milk cart, then rush out to meet the milkman. I recalled the good old days when I would collect cream from the farmer and lick the cream that spilled out of the can. I would long for those exciting days.

On my ninth birthday, Mum gave me a meccano set. It must have cost a lot of money. The rotating motors and the whirling gears thrilled me, so I spent much of my time building cranes, motors and trucks. I had an inventive mind, and mechanics never ceased to fill me with wonder. They kept me engrossed especially on rainy days when I was not allowed to wander on the beach.

Not long after this, Mum complained of stomach pains and would bend forward in her chair with a groan. Once, when I returned from school, I heard her vomiting in the bathroom. Within a few days, the whites of her eyes turned yellow, and her temperature shot up.

Dad took Mum to the hospital. I didn't know how long she'd be away. *Will she ever return? Will she die?* The thought of Mum dying frightened me. I missed her praises when I had constructed something new with my meccano set. I missed seeing her wave me goodbye as I left for school. I miss her lovingly prepared sandwiches. I missed her hot breakfasts.

Mum returned from hospital after a week and I greeted her with joy.

Dad placed his hand upon my shoulder. 'Your Mum has just had her gall bladder taken out, so be careful not to hurt her.'

The warmth of his hand comforted me, but I guessed there was something terribly wrong. 'May I have a look at where the doctor cut you, Mum?' I asked.

She opened the buttons of her blouse and lifted the dressing on her stomach. The wound was red and had black stitches sewn into her flesh.

After her stay in hospital, Mum remained in bed late every morning and didn't prepare breakfast for us anymore. She would put sixpence on the table before retiring for the night. 'That's for your lunch. I don't have the energy to prepare your sandwich.'

Dad left for work after a cup of coffee for breakfast, because he had to start early. Before leaving, he ruffled my hair and said, 'Help yourself to cereals and milk.'

I didn't feel like having breakfast alone, so I grabbed the money and dashed off to school without a bite. For lunch, I bought potato chips from the town fish-and-chip shop, tore the top off the newspaper-wrapping and dived into the pack of hot chips. I enjoyed the chips but they left me hungry and unsatisfied.

Soon, the novelty of buying my own lunch wore off. Home was not like before. I couldn't understand the change in my mother and longed for her love and care. Dad worked seven days a week as a builder and as a wharfie at nights. On his return from work in the evenings, he prepared our evening meal, had dinner, and went to bed for a few hours before setting out for his night shift.

Those were lonely nights. The days were scarcely any better. The milkman left bottles of milk at the main gate of our school, and two boys from each class carried them in. I would volunteer for the chore because my stomach growled from hunger. Once, I gulped down a whole bottle on the way back to class, and when our teacher handed out one bottle to each of us for the morning break, still hungry, I lined up with the rest and took my second drink.

The next day, my nose filled with mucus. I carried several handkerchiefs to school, but they were all full by the end of the day. Soon, I developed a blocked nose and couldn't breathe. I longed to breathe freely once more and dreamed of using a corkscrew to pull out a hard green and yellow cork that blocked my breathing.

'Mum, I cannot breathe through my nose!' I said, trying to speak normally, but my voice sounded nasal.

I met a wall of silence. Either my mother didn't hear me, or she had her own pain to deal with and didn't possess the energy to help me.

As an adult, I learned that I had intolerance to milk and had suffered from an infected sinus as a child. I also came to realise the trauma of a gallbladder operation and the long convalescence it entailed.

Mum returned to work after a few months but life was never the same after her operation.

Formerly, she had suffered from mood swings, but now they grew worse and she didn't appear to care for me any longer. Whenever I fell and hurt myself, she no longer tended my injuries or fussed over me. Instead, she'd say, 'Go to the medicine cabinet and put some iodine on the cut.'

Mum's indifference hurt me. I looked for comfort elsewhere and grew closer to Dad. All the burden of household duties now fell on him. He cooked our tea when he returned from work, had his evening meal, then went to the docks to work as a wharfie. I had to go straight home from school, cut the wood, light the stove and put the kettle on for tea.

Dad bought me a willow cricket bat and encouraged me to play cricket with Jimmy and some other friends, so I joined my mates for a game of cricket in the paddock. We used an old tree stump as the wicket and had great fun, defending our stumps with our lives.

After a game, I'd wipe every trace of grime off my bat and store it in a safe place. I kept it close to me at nights. In the mornings, I stroked it with pride, before leaving for school.

Chapter 9

I WAS BOUNCING IN THE back seat of our car from both excitement and the rough road. We were heading to the Newtons, who farmed a thousand-acre property off the main highway to Hamilton. We had met them in the early fifties when Dad worked for the farming community, and the thought of seeing our old friends again, filled me with excitement.

Three generations lived on the farm—the grandparents, Pa and Ma Newton, their son John and his wife, Phyllis, with their two boys, Ernie and Geordie. The Newtons kept dairy cattle and some pigs. They also had an apple orchard, a few pear trees and an old quince tree.

In the distance, about two miles off, their apple orchard stretched from the top of a hill to the railway-line at the bottom. The perfume from the apple blossoms drifted all the way down to us and the wind played soft music with their leaves.

Dad drove on the gravel road and crossed the railway line that ran to Portland. Giant cypress pines marked the boundary between Newton's farm and the next. Outside the huge wooden gates, a milk can and a small cream can sat on a stand, ready for the butter factory truck. Off to the left, a large box on stilts with the letters R.M.B. 16, housed the mail.

'What's R.M.B?' I asked Mum.

'Royal Mail Bag,' she replied.

What does the Queen have to do with this letterbox when she didn't live anywhere near? I longed to know the answer to my question but Mum had slumped back in her seat and shut her eyes. I knew she was in no mood to talk, so I dared not disturb her any further.

The driveway led to a brown weatherboard house enclosed by a picket fence. The garden was profuse with roses, hollyhocks and petunias, without an inch of space for a blade of grass. Surrounded by acres of pastures, what was the need of a lawn?

My first instinct was to find Pa Newton. I knew I'd find him feeding his pigs. While my parents entered the house, I took the concrete path to the old homestead that now served as a store shed. I tiptoed in. The place was dusty and dark. Cobwebs hung from the ceiling. I shuddered, half-expecting a ghost to glide across. My hair stood on end and goosebumps appeared on my arms.

I threaded my way down the gloomy hallway. One room was used solely for storing the apples. The two largest rooms contained bran and skim-milk for stockfeed. Pa stored the skim-milk in old coppers and lined them up like soldiers along the path that ran through the cluttered back yard. He'd mix the bran and skim-milk into a mash in two huge buckets and carry them to the pig pen.

I ran past rows of kale, cabbages, cauliflowers and carrots that grew in the vegetable garden. Pa leant over the fence and poured the pig-feed into small troughs of hollowed-out logs that lay just inside the pigsty.

The pigs guzzled the slops, doing a pee or a bog in their food at the same time.

Pa watched the pigs feed, then turned and smiled. His smile lit up his entire face. 'Come and have something to eat, lad,' he drawled.

My heart leapt as it always did when Pa Newton smiled.

After a bite of something, I used to wander off with the two boys in search of plover nests. We handled the eggs tenderly, taking no more than one from each nest so that the mother bird would not be too distressed. Ernie and Geordie had quite a collection of eggshells of varying sizes and colours from the local fauna.

During my visits, Pa Newton taught me the delicate art of 'blowing.' He taught me many other things as well. I particularly recall the time I learned about drunken parrots. One day, as I cycled back from school, a Major Mitchell parrot staggered along the path, squawking and reeling like the town drunk.

I told Pa Newton about it the next day. 'I came across a parrot that stumbled along the road. Thinking it was sick, I stuffed the bird in my shirt, cycled home and put it in a cardboard box. You should've seen the mess in my room the next morning. The bird had knocked everything off the shelves and the cupboard. I couldn't catch it, so I opened the window to let it fly off. My room stank of bird poo so Mum went crook at me.'

Pa Newton shook his head. 'Parrots love eating overripe hawthorn berries. It makes them drunk. You'll learn, boy. You'll learn more about the country as time passes.'

When the apple trees in the orchard were heavy with ripe fruit, we clambered up the branches and placed the pickings in large laundry baskets. Then we gently lowered them to waiting hands. Finally, we sorted and stored the apples for winter.

If there were no fruit to be picked, we would clamber up ten feet tall saplings for fun. The leaves caressed us and the tree bent over, leaving us dangling. We hung on until it smacked on the ground and a loud sound like the crack of a rifle shot exploded as the trunk broke off. We scrambled up the next one and repeated the process. Our antics kept the paddocks free of trees and allowed the grass to grow for the stock. Pa Newton knew every one of his herd of seventy and named each after a flower. I especially recall Daisy and Daffodil, Buttercup and Petunia.

The holding yard had a concrete floor, and we boys would drive round and round the enclosure in a pedal car, dodging among the animals.

No matter how far off we were, when we heard a 'Cooee,' it was like rattling a feed bucket in front of the poddy calves. We dropped everything, raced back to the farm house and went straight to the dining room. A table left barely enough space to walk around three sides. On one side, Ma Newton had placed a bench against the wall and we kids had to slide along to get to our places. Once we were seated, the ladies laid the table and brought out the food. My mouth would water and my stomach would growl.

Like most farming people, Ma Newton could not tolerate the sight of a skinny person, and kept filling my plate. We had cake or scones for morning tea. Her speciality looked like an upside-down mushroom. She kept the recipe a secret. My favourite, a thick slice of homemade bread soaked in jam and cream, oozed into my open mouth. Its creamy sweetness melted, slow and delicious. It danced around my tongue before sliding down my throat. The cake not only tasted good. It was sublime.

Ma Newton and her daughter-in-law grew parcels of parsnips, pea and, beans, potatoes and pumpkins, Brussel sprouts and broccoli and beets. For dinner, they cooked whatever was in season at the time. The aroma of their roast meat never failed to rouse my appetite.

The days were hardly ever long enough for me. I loved their way of life so much that I vowed to grow most of my vegetables when I grew up.

On Thursdays, Old Pa went to town in his utility. Years back, he drove his horse and sulky that he now stored in a lean-to against the hayshed. He had four types of old and dusty one-horse carriages in the shed. During the summer holidays, Ernie, Geordie and I would pull the smallest one into the paddock and race around with one of us on each shaft. The third sat back in the seat with his hands behind his head or his fingers laced over his belly. We took turns to have a ride, re-living the horse-and-buggy days.

The regular horses had long gone but Pa Newton still kept two elephant-sized Clydesdales. We'd sit astride their broad backs, then slide down and walk around, patting their flanks or stroking their noses.

Pa Newton constructed a sledge of two tree trunks with a wooden plank deck, and used it when heavy rains made the ground too soft for a tractor. After he attached a chain to each end, away the horses would go, with Pa walking along, holding the reins. The sledge just glided like a skater skimming on ice.

During inclement weather, we sheltered in the barn and enjoyed the odour of hay, horses and manure. At times, we built passages and rooms with bales of hay or lay down and dozed off.

One morning while playing in the barn, I lost the pocketknife I'd received for attending Sunday school. My heart sank. I knew I'd never be able to replace it. We searched for hours, shifting bales of hay and peering into every nook and cranny but found no trace of my penknife. At lunch-time, we told Ma and Pa Newton of my loss, and after the meal, we rushed back to continue our search.

When Ma Newton called us in for afternoon tea, Pa asked if my knife had turned up.

I shook my head and fought back tears, clenching my teeth to prevent the sobs from escaping. 'May I leave the table and search for it again?'

'No.' Pa Newton sounded hoarse. He didn't have a bad throat, but perhaps he too wanted to weep for me. His tightly compressed lips opened slightly as if he was about to say something, but they closed again.

I turned away desolate. Each time I put my hand into my pocket and the penknife wasn't there, I groaned in agony. I bemoaned my loss and, for the next few weeks, I continued my search.

A month later, Pa handed me a packet tied with a blue ribbon. 'I found it when tossing the hay.'

I untied the bow with trembling hands. Inside was the red penknife—sharp and shiny. I grasped it to my chest. 'Thank you, Pa. I really cannot thank you enough. Where did you find it?'

His eyes twinkled and he gazed at me before speaking. Then his smile broadened. 'Sitting on top of a hay stack.'

Years later, Mum told me that Pa Newton had bought a new knife and pretended to have discovered it in the barn. I was not surprised. Pa was a man who would do the world for you without expecting any thanks.

On weekends, I would take the shortcut from my house and follow the railway line, skipping along the sleepers or balancing on the lines until I came to the farm. When his two grandsons were away at boarding school, I had many delightful hours alone with Pa Newton. I followed the old man with the dog-like devotion of a lonely boy and worked on the land or rambled about the property.

Besides teaching me all about dairy farming, Pa Newton encouraged me. 'Be a land-owner when you grow up.'

I ran my hand through my hair and scratched my head like Pa did when thinking. 'We have no money.'

'Don't worry. Borrow some and repay the loan from the farm produce.'

How easy it all seemed. At times, I dreamed of joining the Navy or running away to live as a hermit in the bush, but the longing to own a property persisted.

One day at my autumn break, Ernie and Geordie Newton, who were already back from boarding school, came to meet me. I hefted my school bag to my shoulder and mounted my bike. We cycled to their grandfather's farm to help pick the fruit. On our way, we passed their herd of dairy cows chewing on the lush grass.

'Do *you* know their names?' I asked.

They shook their heads. I was amazed. By then I knew all their names, just like Pa did.

Panting, we rode halfway up the hill and dismounted, pushing our bikes the rest of the way. We leaned them against the white picket fence and entered the garden, where we were greeted by the perfume of roses.

The two boys ran into the weatherboard house, but I raced over to the old homestead. Pa Newton usually worked there, and I couldn't wait to see him again. I tiptoed in, hoping to surprise him. Musty and dusty cobwebs hung from the ceiling. I passed the apple storeroom and glanced in. No one. On I went, past the coppers lined up like soldiers beside the path. I streaked along the backyard to the pig pen. *Perhaps he's feeding the pigs?*

He wasn't there either. *By now, he should have long finished the morning milking. Where is he? Is he ill?* I raced back to the family home and mounted the steps, two at a time.

Pa Newton beamed at me. 'Where've you been, Colin?'

'Looking for you,' I gasped.

'Time for lunch and relaxing with *Blue Hills*,' the old man said.

How foolish I am! At home, I always listen to my favourite programme, but I must've forgotten because I wanted to see him so much.

After a lunch of homemade bread, fresh butter and cold roast pork, Pa Newton stretched out his arm to switch on the radio. He rubbed the left side of his chest, groaned and leaned back to listen to the next episode of *Blue Hills*. We gathered around.

When it was over, he staggered over to the verandah and picked up a spade.

Ma Newton followed him. 'Why don't you try the new toilet? It'll save you a walk to the bush in this heat.'

'Change isn't healthy. You ladies can use the septic system if you like.' He trudged off.

We boys looked at each other and chuckled. I loved to sit comfortably in the loo and pull the chain to flush the toilet. What luxury!

I usually followed Pa when he called his cows in for afternoon milking. He always stroked each animal and spoke gently to them. One day however, I had to help gather in the rest of the apples.

When the boys and I returned burdened with fruit, Pa pointed to a basket of overripe fruit. 'Take this with you and feed the pigs. And don't pelt them with it.'

We ran off, and as soon as we were out of his sight, we started bombarding the pigs. They squealed and snorted, dodging our missiles.

The commotion must have reached Pa, because on our return his brow furrowed. 'Did you disobey me?' His frown was like a dark cloud and shut off the rays of joy that he radiated.

A sense of guilt stole over me and I mumbled, 'Sorry, Pa.'

Disappointment showed in his eyes. 'That was cruel. Go and catch possums if you want to do something useful. They've been eating our fruit and playing havoc with the vegetables. Take Bluey with you.'

Pa Newton had five cattle dogs on the farm. Bluey, the favourite, followed us everywhere. When we were in the paddock, he sniffed around an electric-fence post and cocked his leg. A charge hit him in his tender parts as urine spurted on the live wire. Bluey yelped and leaped three feet into the air. Then he turned upon the fence, growling and snarling. As soon as his moist nose touched the line, Bluey howled in pain and disbelief.

After a few minutes, he bounded into Ernie's arms.

'The poor mutt. I bet he'll never go near that place again,' Ernie said, hugging Bluey to his chest and rubbing his neck.

Geordie and I rolled on the ground in hysterics then raced back to tell Pa about Bluey. *He'd forgive us for not having caught any possums and laugh over the incident.* I couldn't wait to hear his full-throated roar and see him slapping his thigh with glee.

The cows were lowing as we approached the dairy. Not all had been milked, but there was no sign of Pa. Filled with unnamed foreboding, we took off for the house.

I entered the cottage before the others. Pa lay on the floor, his right hand stretched out. His left hand clutched his heart. The phone dangled from its cord. I sprang to his side and felt his pulse. There was no response from him.

'Pa. Pa,' I cried.

My words fell on deaf ears. He stared at us with unseeing eyes.

John and the two ladies were out shopping. No one else was at home. *How ironic it is that Pa, who detested new-fangled things, had been reaching out for the telephone to get help!*

Sobs tore my chest, ripping my heart into shreds.

I'll never forget the lessons old Pa Newton taught me. From him, I learned to be gentle with animals. From him I learned to be helpful to others. From him I learned to love the land. I knew I'd never be satisfied until I owned my own plot of land, and kept poultry and grew fruit and vegetables.

In 2005, I returned to Portland with my wife. By then, Ma Newton had also died and only their children remained.

The place was in ruins. Horses roamed freely in what was left of the orchard. They had eaten everything, leaving only bare skeletons of trees.

I shut my eyes, visualising the apple-laden branches, then I pressed a fist against my mouth and mumbled, 'The boys never did like farming.'

With a trembling chin and eyelids heavy with unshed tears, I hurried my wife back to the car, leaving the farm to its ghosts.

Chapter 10

PORTLAND'S CHARACTERS WERE UNFORGETTABLE. One in particular, stood out from the rest. Slobberer Dawkins had an air of mystery about him. Dirty and unshaven, he wore a black trilby and an army overcoat that must have been used during the Great War. He'd been educated at a public school in England and had an Oxford accent, yet he never put on airs or graces.

Dawkins and his brother lived some six or seven miles out of Portland and raised pigs. The younger brother always remained at home while Dawkins drove a horse and a four-wheeled dray to collect slops. He often parked the cart and sat with his head fallen forward; hands holding the reins while his horse munched chaff from its nosebag. Everyone called him Slobberer, and ostracised him because of his dirty and untidy appearance, but Mum insisted I address him as Mr Dawkins.

He sometimes overtook us on our way home from town and, doffing his hat, he'd offer us a ride. Mum never failed to clamber in and thank him over and over again. My face grew warm as I climbed into the cart, grateful for the lift even though my nose twitched at the sour smell of the scraps.

One day, when Dad and I were looking at cars in a car yard, Mr Dawkins strode up to a salesman. 'What's the cost of a brand-new truck?'

The clerk picked his teeth and stared at the filthy figure before him. Looking him up and down, he said, 'You can't afford to buy one, mate.'

Mr Dawkins left the premises without a word.

Dad nudged me. 'Let's see what he does now!'

We followed at a respectable distance.

Mr Dawkins approached another dealer and placed a dirty hand on the bonnet of a shiny new lorry. 'I'll have this one.'

The sales clerk didn't bat an eyelid at Slobberer's dirty and worn clothes. 'You may drive away in the truck if you have the money, mate.'

The pig-breeder glanced at the price pasted on the windshield and delved deep into the recesses of his stinking overcoat. Pulling out a wad of notes, he peeled them off one by one until he had the exact amount. He did it with finesse, then signed the necessary papers and drove off with the lorry.

When Dad told Mum about it she put her hands upon her hips. 'Serves that first salesman right! Didn't I tell you to treat Mr Dawkins with respect?'

That was my first practical lesson to be polite to everyone regardless of their standing in the community.

Another interesting character was Jimmy Schofield, an English Jew who was one of the first people Dad came to know in Portland. He owned the local C.O.R. (now B.P) petrol station, which stocked everything from pins and needles to steel girders. When petrol was still rationed in Australia, Jimmy sold Dad a car and supplied us with a forty-four-gallon drum at a discount rate.

He placed his index finger to his nose and lowered his voice. 'You're a primary producer because you live in a farmhouse.'

Dad nodded knowingly. He made a stand for the drum and drained the petrol into the tank of our car. He continued this procedure until post-war rationing ceased.

Dad often took me hunting with his friend, Harold, who owned a utility. Dad drove the vehicle, and I sat in the back with Harold. Whenever a rabbit came into view, Harold would raise his rifle and shoot it. He rarely missed. Dad would stop the car and I'd jump out, race to the rabbit and put it in a sack.

I learned to shoot during these hunting trips and always longed to own a rifle. On my twelfth birthday, Dad presented me with a long parcel. *Is it a fishing rod?* I already had a home-made one. Hands trembling, I tore off the wrapping. Inside was a Twenty-two!

'Now, remember all the things you've learned about handling a gun and don't ever point it at anyone,' Dad said.

I flung my arms around him. 'Thanks, Dad.'

'Go along then and try it out,' he said.

Jimmy Schofield sold his shots at five shillings six pence a packet of fifty. I ran off, taking the shortest route to his store. I glanced at his price tag and shook my head. 'The butter factory co-op down the road sells them for *less*.'

Jimmy jerked his head sideways. 'You buy your bullets here, lad, and I'll meet their price.'

I bought the bullets and raced out to test my rifle.

An English family who ran the corner-store converted their shop into a self-service store—the first anyone had ever seen. The building was nothing more than a fibro shed with a double door. Not much larger than today's corner-store, it had shelves down each side and a double-sided shelf in the centre. The flat metal roof turned it into a furnace in summer and an iceberg in winter. The bare concrete floor was level with the footpath. The road camber fell away with no kerb or gutters for drainage, so when it rained, the floors flooded.

One day, Mum sent me to buy some biscuits. I swaggered down to the store, whistling a tune, delighted to hear the jingle of coins in my pocket. The shop-assistant fetched a pair of scales, took down a large biscuit tin, and weighed the required amount.

Shopping was an excuse for an outing, and families would stop for a chat. On Thursdays, farmers crowded into town and purchase goods from the Co-op. No one accepted cheques because they invariably bounced. Not that folk meant to be dishonest, but times were hard, and they waited for good crops before paying their debts.

A solicitor, who served a jail sentence at Ararat for fiddling the books, was another interesting Portland character. His case was an example of greed.

During his time in jail, he won the first prize at a singing competition by performing the popular song: *I was a big man yesterday, but boy; you want to see me now!*

People never stopped saying, 'He was a fool to embezzle money and throw away such a good career.'

This incident re-enforced my belief in the importance of honesty.

Mr Small, an estate agent who had made his fortune manufacturing Malvern Star bicycles, never failed to help the elderly and less fortunate.

Dad met him at a Salvation Army Meeting, where Mr Small played the tenor horn. The Salvos had helped soldiers during the war, so Dad and Bruce Small became good friends.

I'll never forget the time Bruce Small sold all he had and departed for the coast south of Brisbane to build a new town. I was about twelve at the time he sold his holding in Allied Bruce Small and dropped in to say goodbye.

Before he left, he told Dad, 'You can buy land there for next to nothing. It'll be worth a mint in years to come. That's where the money is—not here.'

Dad scratched his head and his eyes gleamed. 'I wouldn't mind making a fortune, but let me think about it.'

He consulted his friends about the idea of joining Bruce Small.

'The area is mostly sand dunes and swamps. Full of mozzies and sand flies,' a friend said. 'He'll never make a go of it. You know what real estate fellows are like. Always flogging off worthless land at a huge profit.'

The town is now known as Surfers Paradise on Queensland's Gold Coast. Bruce Small worked his way up the ladder and was elected mayor of the city in 1967. He died of cancer in Benowa. Six years after his death, his role in the development of the Gold Coast was officially recognised and his statue was erected in Elkhorn Avenue, Surfers Paradise.

Had Dad followed the entrepreneur's advice, he may have made a fortune too, but he was cautious and remained in Portland until he found a steady job in Canberra.

Years later, I dabbled in the Share Market. I did well at first, but after the stock market crash in October 2008, I withdrew with grace. Fortunately, I didn't fare as badly as many of my contemporaries did. I had learned from Dad to be prudent and not gamble away my hard-earned cash.

I admired country folk for their frankness. If anyone wanted to know the latest gossip, they went to Kacker Dustan, the town barber.

Whenever people wanted a job done Dad consulted him in case they turned out to be a bad risk.

Dad said, 'What Kacker don't know isn't worth knowing.' A swinging door, like the batwing doors in cowboy movies led into his shop. It had two chairs. One was reserved for the customer, and the other for anyone who cared to drop in for a chat.

Kacker would lean against the doorway with an arm on his hip when work was slack. 'G'day, mate,' he would sing out to every passer-by.

Nine years after we left Portland for Canberra, I called in at the old place. Kacker Duston stood in the same posture as before, greeting people as they passed his shop.

'G'day, Colin,' he drawled, as though I'd never left the town.

I strode over to him and shook his hand, surprised he hadn't forgotten me. I must have changed considerably, having grown up from a lanky fourteen-year-old, to a broad shouldered young man in my twenties. I went in for a haircut, but mainly to catch up with the latest gossip.

When I returned to Portland with my wife three decades later to launch her book, *Where's Home Mummy,* he was no longer there. To my regret, I was unable to find out what became of some of the people who'd helped shape my early years.

Kacker Duston had a younger brother who sold fish. One Saturday morning during the peak hour, he wheeled his barrow of fresh fish before him, crying, 'Fresh cockles and mussels, alive, alive, oh!'

A new police constable from Melbourne, who had replaced our popular constable, Andy, decided to use the strong arm of the law. He took out his notebook and pen.

'What are you booking me for?' the hawker asked, with an innocent look on his face.

The policeman took a step forward and towered over him. 'For wheeling your barrow on the wrong side of the road!'

Young Duston glared at him. 'How do you know that?' Then he took up his barrow and *pulled* it behind him.

I saw that he was now facing the left side, and was on the correct side of the road! The constable's face turned as red as the bricks on the pavement. He pocketed his notebook and left amid the laughter and catcalls of the onlookers.

The police often called Dad in for small jobs on their police station, and I used to accompany him and play in the empty cells. Around Christmas one year, Dad was requested to build a chimney and stove in the police quarters, so he drove straight to the station after work, and parked his vehicle outside. He was about to enter the building, when the new constable strode out to our car and walked right round it.

He kicked the tyres. 'They're bald and need replacing.' He slid his hand into his pocket and fumbled for his notebook. He must have sworn to conduct a vendetta on the townsfolk for laughing at him over the barrow incident.

Dad snatched up his tools and stomped towards the door. 'You book my car and there'll be no fireplace and chimney to bake your Christmas turkey!'

The constable's face grew red. 'Just get along with the job. I was only *warning* you.'

I admired Dad for not letting himself be bullied and for putting the man in his place. Later, as an adult, I too, wouldn't allow anyone to intimidate me simply because he held a position of authority.

Not long after this, much to the delight of the townsfolk, the new cop was recalled, and our own popular policeman, Andy, returned to Portland.

Andy had a sense of humour. On one occasion three workmen who had been working at a traffic intersection, decided to play a joke on their mate. They trussed him up in a wheel barrow and placed it near the raised dome or the *Silent Policeman,* as we called it.

The constable stopped his car next to the *Silent Policeman* on the intersection and wound down the window. 'Are you all right, mate?'

'The boys were just having a bit of fun,' the victim answered, probably hoping the constable would untie him.

He didn't. Instead, he drove off chuckling, leaving others to rescue the poor man.

A few days later, a shop owner at the top-end of town—meaning up the hill, not the posh part—phoned the Police Station, reporting that someone had used his front entrance as a toilet. The shop stood next to the Royal Hotel and the door was set back about three feet, creating a dark recess at nights.

On inspection, the police constable found that the local town drunk had indeed used it as a toilet. Flies buzzed around something round and brown. Taking care not to step on the faeces, the policeman rubbed his nose.

The shop-owner's voice rose. He shook his fist. 'Lock the bastard up. It's not fair!'

The constable nodded. 'I'll look into this. Meanwhile, if no one claims it in seven days, you may keep it.'

When Dad told us this, I chuckled at the policeman's sense of humour, but felt that the guilty man should have been made to clean up the mess.

The most striking person I ever met in Portland was Lady Smyth. Townsfolk said she'd met the Queen. In those days, people spoke of Her Majesty with respect.

Dad, however, used to say, 'She's a silly old fart. *I* fought in the war while she stayed at home.'

Sometimes, I sneaked into the gardens of a grand mansion to look at the goldfish. The house had a glassed-in veranda, and the garden appeared like something out of a magazine, with green lawns, colourful flowerbeds and well-trimmed hedges. Even in the most inclement weather, I'd stop and watch the goldfish and try to scoop up the big ones with my hands.

One fine day, I stopped to admire the fish. I had nothing to fear. Only rarely did I catch glimpses of a gardener.

Sprays of jasmine tumbled from the top of an arbour and covered a rock wall. The pond contained fishes of all shades of red and orange. Their rainbow hues glinted in the sunlight, changing colours like chameleons.

I glimpsed a reflection on the water and looked up.

Lady Smyth stood before me at the opposite end of the pond. Her grey hair was neatly combed back into a bun. She wore a light muslin dress and stared at me from beneath her parasol.

I'd once been caught stealing apples from an orchard, and the local policeman had dragged me home by the ear. Mum's frown had been like a thundercloud drifting into the clear blue sky of my happiness and was even more painful than Dad's hiding.

Now, as if a wicked fairy had waved a wand over me, the goldfish turned to crown-of-thorns fish. Fish that tore my insides to shreds. Fish that had caused me to trespass on another's property. Fish that would lead to my ruin.

'Who are you?' The voice was gentle.

'Colin Barker,' I stammered, hoping the ground would open and swallow me.

'I know your mother. She used to do some light duties for me.'

I clasped my hands and waited, breathless.

Lady Smyth placed her hand on my shoulder and led me indoors. 'Come into my house and look at my museum.'

The crown-of-thorns ceased their clawing, and I followed, eager to see what lay ahead.

The mansion was a magical place, showing glimpses of far-off lands. Buffaloes' heads and stags' horns gaped at me from polished boards on the walls. A tiger skin complete with its head, bared its teeth from the centre of the room.

Lady Smyth's soft tones cast a spell over me. 'My husband has been in that exotic land of Kipling's. A tiger had been stalking the locals and killing their cattle. They appealed for help, so he hunted down the beast.' She glanced at the fur rug on her polished floor. 'The villagers presented the skin as a trophy.'

I gasped and, in my childish eyes, I saw her husband seated on an elephant, firing his rifle as the tiger leapt towards him.

Another room had a table of polished oak and glass cabinets containing bright red uniforms, purple sashes, swords and spears, hatchets and relics from Burma—that land of pagodas and flying fish. The room was spotless, and the smell of polish rose from the floor. Brass handles on the cabinets shone like gold. Later, as a sea cadet, I realised that it was a typical officers' mess.

A show cabinet containing the Victoria Cross caught my attention. I held my hands to my mouth and gazed and gazed. Finally, I plucked up my courage. 'Did the Brigadier win this?'

'In 1915, my husband was a young officer,' Lady Smyth said. 'He and ten others were carrying ammunition to the soldiers at the front line in France. Twenty yards off from the enemy's position, a hail of bullets greeted them.'

With parted lips, I listened. The roar of cannon fire thundered, accompanied by the crack of rifles, raining shrapnel and bullets down like hailstones.

'Only my husband and two soldiers remained standing,' Lady Smyth continued. Tears glistened in her eyes and compassion for her swept over me like a wave.

Burma and Portland must have had some type of mystical connection. Several years later, I met Hazel, who had been born in Mandalay—a meeting destined to shape our lives. From her, I later heard of Brigadier Smyth, who'd fought in Burma during World War II.

I thought of nothing else but my visit to Lady Smyth's house, on my way to school. That evening, I hugged myself and rocked back and forth on my heels. 'Lady Smyth invited me into her home, Mum.'

The very next day, Mum took me over to our neighbour's place.

'Lady Smyth invited my son into her house and showed him her husband's medals!' she boasted. Shards of light shone on her hair as she flipped it back.

Chapter 11

I LOVED LOOKING OUT TO SEA and watching the fishing fleet leave port on a ten-foot swell. Each ship's silhouette against the evening sky was a familiar sight. I knew every vessel by name. The harbour had a timber jetty for unloading the catch. My mates and I enjoyed cleaning and tidying the boats when they came in. The stench of diesel oil mingled with the odour of rotting fish, while we worked, and the cry of the ever-squabbling sea gulls drowned the sound of waves lapping on the shore.

As a reward for our help, the fishermen gave us enough fish to last a whole week and also tossed in a few under-sized crayfish if no inspector was around.

One Sunday, when a couple of his crew had gone down with influenza, the skipper offered to take us out to the fishing grounds. My insides vibrated with joy and a wide grin spread over my face as I slipped the mooring ropes and sprang on board.

The captain taught us how to grab the float that identified his craypot locations and haul up the ones he'd left out the previous night. This wasn't as easy as it looked, because the waves kept pushing them away. When the rope finally lay neatly coiled on deck like a snake, we stored the saleable crayfish in a seawater-filled hold and threw the unwanted *debris* back into the sea. Finally, we pushed a wire through a stinking fish and tied it down as bait, making sure the crays would have to enter the trap before reaching it.

After six hours of lifting and re-laying pots, the skipper went down below with the others to pack the cray, leaving me alone to steer the ship home. A sense of power and elation overwhelmed me. I grasped the tiller, proud of being in absolute control of the vessel. The deep-throated thud of the diesel motor and the joy of running up a wave and down the other side, overwhelmed me. I longed to own a boat someday.

About midnight we approached the harbour, and the captain took over from me and docked the boat. One of the crew dropped me home.

My blood still surging in a rich afterglow, I forgot I'd been out since early morning, until I opened our front door and saw a dozen men drinking beer or dragging on their fags. They stared at me as though I was a water sprite with my wet clothes.

A rough-looking man with a scar face put down his glass and glared at me. 'Since dark, we've been searching for the body of a lad about your age.'

I didn't like his menacing tone and stepped back from him, seeking shelter behind Dad, whose face had turned a bright red.

'Thank you mates,' Dad said. I'd never seen him drunk, so his heightened colour must have come from anger.

A man banged his fist on the table before leaving. Others drained their glasses and drifted off.

The look on Mum's face was ominous. She glanced at Dad.

I knew I was in for a thrashing and quickly devised a plan to avert punishment.

Taking a step forward, I placed the bag of cray into my mother's hands. 'This is for us, Mum.'

The ruse worked. Mum smiled and took the bag into the kitchen. Perhaps I needed less attention than the crayfish.

The coastline consisted of tall cliffs and stretches of sandy beaches and kelp-covered rocks. Local fishermen converged on the area, as it was the best place for rock-fishing in Portland. Behind them were golden mimosa and red bottle brush. Brilliant birds of the bush added to their charm. Further inland, lay farmland and forests of hardwood timber.

In time, sand drifts marched on, menacing properties, and turning them into sand dunes. I enjoyed sliding down them, then clawing my way back uphill.

One Sunday when exploring the beach, a forty-four-gallon petrol container bounced on the water. The waves gradually brought it closer to shore, so I sped home on my bicycle and panted out the news to Dad.

He grabbed his car keys and a coil of rope, then drove down to the foreshore. His muscles bulged as he fought with the waves, trying to drag the drum to shore. While Dad re-gained his breath, and waves threatened to carry it back to sea, I threw my body against it to hold the drum back.

It took the best part of the day to retrieve the drum. Exhausted and soaking wet, we used a plank to roll it into the boot of the car, and drove home.

Once back, Dad opened the bung and sniffed. *Petrol*. What a prize!

He didn't stop talking about his luck for months. I'd been a hero. I immersed myself in the glory.

One day a friend leaned towards Dad, as though telling a secret, and said, 'A storm probably swept it off a ship.'

My ears pricked up. *What else could I find?*

One weekend while staying at Uncle Doug's house, I went beach-combing again, scouting for treasures. The wind buffeted me as I scanned the horizon. The sand bit like shards of glass and the sun burned me, but oblivious of the scorching heat, I kept looking even though my eyes hurt.

Through a blur of tears, I saw something bobbing up and down in the distance. *Is it a dolphin at play or is it a shark?* I waited. *If only I had a telescope.* I rolled my hands in the shape of one and peered through. Nothing. I twisted my head back and forth, scanning every inch of water where I'd last seen the object.

Another forty-four-gallon drum floated on the surface. The waves brought my booty closer to shore. *Aviation fuel.* I spelled out the words.

Barely ten at the time but tall, thin and wiry, I raced into the water and seized my prize. The ocean roared and leapt like a lion unwilling to release its prey. I clung on, but a wall of surf raced towards me and knocked me off my feet. I staggered to the beach, coughing and gasping like a fish caught in a net.

Once I had regained my breath, I stepped into the water again and watched each incoming wave bringing the treasure closer to the beach, which was covered by fist-sized rocks that formed a steep slope.

When I finally grasped the aviation fuel, I jammed the drum securely among a pile of rocks and sped off.

Aunt Barbara sat knitting in the garden.

'I've got a drum of petrol!' My words were hoarse.

She put down her knitting and stared at me in obvious disbelief. 'What? Another one?'

'Yes, another one.'

'Well, why don't you bring it home?'

'It's too heavy to carry.'

'Then empty it into the sea.'

Her voice held a tone of authority in it and sounded like a challenge. *I'll show her. I'll show her I did find a treasure. I'll show her I'm not lying.*

I raced back. My wet shorts clung to my legs. Salt water stung my eyes. I wrestled with the plug, pulled it out and emptied the precious contents.

At first, a dirty black pool appeared; within minutes, the dark patch grew menacing and turned green and blue as it spread over the water. Then the strong smell of petrol polluted the atmosphere.

Rolling the empty drum before me, I made my way back. The gate clicked as I kicked it shut. Clothes drenched in oil, I stood before Aunt Barbara with the prize.

The look on her face told me she realised I'd been speaking the truth. She put down her knitting and rose from her seat. 'Go and have a hot shower.' Her voice trembled.

When Dad heard of the incident, he glared at his sister-in-law, shook his head and banged his fist on the table. 'Your aunt has thrown away our chance of making a quick buck.'

A few days later, a friend of Dad's who had an air pilot's licence, threw up his hands in despair when he heard our story. 'Aviation fuel is hard to get and is *very* expensive. I'd have brought a crane and a truck to get the drum and paid you good money.'

Fortunately, Aunt Barbara wasn't present. From the look on Dad's face, I think he may have throttled her.

Dad must have had an affinity for petrol. One day while filling the car at the petrol-pump, he told me a story of his tenth wedding anniversary. For weeks, Mum had been hinting about a gift. She'd been longing for the famous English Redboy chocolates, and meant to store some letters in the tin, after eating the chocolate.

Dad had been busy overhauling his car, when Mum again reminded him of their anniversary. After fixing the vehicle, he drove down to the pub in his dirty overalls.

On his return, without removing his muddy boots, Dad staggered into our spotless dining room. He held out a five-gallon tin of petrol to Mum. 'Here's your anniversary gift.'

He placed it on the table and turned, leaving smudge marks on the floor. He never liked being disturbed when working in the garage, and obviously meant to teach Mum a lesson.

'Your mother was not amused,' he said. I noticed a gleam of satisfaction in his eyes when he told me the story.

Dad realised he could earn more money as a wharfie, so after gaining his stevedore's ticket, he worked the nightshifts. Cargo consisted of bales of wool, frozen lamb from the meat-works or tinned milk from Glaxco's plant, near Port Fairy. At the time, shipping of bulk wheat and live sheep had not yet commenced.

Dad often spoke of his life as a wharfie. 'Coppers stood by, watching us loading and unloading cargo, yet stores keep disappearing from the docks. They could never catch us. In the early hours of the morning when we knock off work, one of us acts as lookout. His job is to throw up his arms and shout, "Search me. I've nothing," whenever a Customs Officer approaches. This is a signal for us to dump our stolen goods into the water. We believed in honour among thieves and always shared the spoils with the lookout who never stole anything.'

At times, Dad returned with tins of butter and bully beef, and rounds of cheese. Then we had bread and butter—and not bread and dripping, which left a coat of grease on my tongue.

Mum sewed clothes for us whenever Dad laid his hands on a roll of material. Once when Dad returned with several rolls of gingham, she said, 'That's just what I need.'

Mum spent the next few weeks, making curtains for the house.

Whenever Dad brought home skeins of wool, Mum knitted thick woollen jumpers for us.

One day, knowing the skipper was not on board, some wharfies donned white overalls and approached a seaman.

Their spokesman said, 'I'd like to see the steward. The captain has asked our firm to tune his piano.'

After fussing with it for an hour, the 'piano tuner' said. 'Afraid it's too big a job. We'll have to take it to the workshop.'

The steward refused permission.

The stevedore spoke in a low, gravelly voice and made a show of packing up his tools. 'We've come in because of an urgent call from your captain. We're terribly busy and will not be back!'

Fearing the skipper's anger, the steward relented, and the piano was carted off.

The captain never saw his piano again.

When Dad was not called up to work on Saturday nights, Mum insisted on going to the movies no matter what was on. I sank down on the seat and enjoyed every film. During the interval, we had lollies and ice-cream and talked to other Poms. I loved those late nights sitting with a bag of sweets, immersed in the unfolding adventures.

If Dad had work on Sunday and could not take us out, I got up early and headed for my favourite haunt, a headland about one or two acres in size. A gravel road ran through stunted heath land and led to a stone quarry. Large creatures had riddled the place with a network of tunnels. Whenever my foot sank into one, I followed its course in the hope of finding the mysterious creature but all my efforts proved futile.

Years later, I learned that the tunnels had been made by heath rats. They could grow up to twelve centimetres in body length and weigh from fifty-five to ninety grams. They had grey-brown fluffy fur with bushy tails.

Unfortunately, they are now a threatened species in Victoria.

I also loved to sit and gaze at the penguins playing hide-and-seek among the waves. Once a pod of whales dived and showed their patterned flukes. Thrilled with excitement, I watched them perform their antics.

St. Lawrence Island stood fifty to a hundred feet above the sea, a mile offshore to the west of Portland. White and aggressive, the ocean lashed the rock, tearing to ribbons any boat that lingered within reach of its jagged teeth. I sat mesmerised, imagining the thirty-three-foot waves smashing into ships and sending up fountains of spray.

Years later, I went there fishing for crayfish with local anglers. Only on dead-calm days did we attempt to get close to the treacherous rock, but even then, we never dared land our craft on the St Lawrence.

In 1853, the outbreak of the Crimean War aroused government interest in fortifying Australia's ports. The Russian scare worsened when, in 1863, the 17-gun Russian corvette *Bogatyr* sailed down the eastern coast to survey Botany Bay. Seven years later, when Britain had withdrawn her garrisons from Sydney, the government decided to build batteries for defending our ports.

In 1889, a gun emplacement and a concrete bunker had been built on a rocky headland to the south of Portland, at Horseshoe Bay to ward off Russian ships. The long barrels on the rearing cliffs sniffed the salty air for enemies, but like most fortifications around the coast of Australia, the guns never fired a shot. The Russians had either been scared off by the cannon or found the tyranny of distance too difficult to overcome.

The rocky outcrop and its battery became known to us as Battery Point. It contained a magazine for storing ammunition and three-gun emplacements. We had no idea whether the magazine contained live ammunition or not. I rarely visited the bunker without my mates, Jim, Derek, Robert and the others. Its leeward side formed the shape of the figure three in mirror reverse. Up to ten feet tall, the sides tailed away to ground level. The seaward section reared up to a height of three feet above the bunker, so the slope provided sufficient space for a high-speed bike race.

We would streak down without touching the brakes until the very last second before reaching the cliff edge, to avoid plunging into the sea. The death-defying ride brought colour to our cheeks and sent thrills down my spine.

One day, feeling in a more adventurous mood, the bigger boys hung on to handholds within the concrete bunker and descended into the dark shafts to the ammunition storage area. Minutes later, a face appeared, covered with cobwebs that held his hair down like Mum's hairnet.

His voice thundered, 'Get out of here. Fast! Unexploded bombs! Could go off anytime.'

Fear wrenched my guts as I fled for the exit with the rest of the group. We never attempted to climb down and explore its depths after that.

By the time I was old enough to probe its secrets, the openings had been bricked up. Now, the underground magazines are not accessible to the public, and a picnic area overlooks the new harbour. The old and rusty guns still remain, the barrels smooth and shiny from our constant straddling them.

After one of the jaunts to Battery Point, I developed a boil on my forearm—big, red and molten—with a yellow crater in the centre. The arm swelled and the pain became excruciating.

Mum held out a black plaster and waved the tarry substance before me. 'This is the best cure. It'll burst the boil and get the pus out.'

After Mum had boiled the plaster, Dad grasped me while she smeared on the ointment. I felt as though a volcano had erupted and covered my arm with molten lava. I struggled to free myself and grit my teeth in a desperate effort to hold back my tears. I squirmed and squealed but Dad held me tight.

'Never hurt Dad.' Mum's voice was soothing but it didn't lessen my pain.

After the torture, she bandaged my arm.

'If boils have more than one head, you call them carbuncles,' Dad said. *He'd know. He had a crop of them the previous year.*

Mum put me to bed later, and sheer exhaustion brought the solace of sleep. The next morning the black goo had drawn the yellow head to the surface of my inflamed skin. Dad encased me in an iron grip and Mum pressed the sides of the boil. The brain-shattering pain seemed to last forever. Then the pus oozed out.

I felt instant relief when a boil burst, spilling its contents on the clean white rag Mum held. 'Yo duttie sod!' Dad would exclaim, looking at the foul-smelling pus.

I would wipe the tears that had sprung to my eyes, glad to escape to my room.

Boils kept cropping up like apples in autumn. Enough for a whole harvest. Each time Mum repeated the procedure, I'd let loose blood-curdling screams, making the house sound like a cinema during a Boris Karloff film.

Among all my adventures, the Billy Cart Derby stood out as the highlight of my primary school days. Dad built a billycart for me, and each year I'd never fail to watch the fun, longing for the time I'd be old enough to race mine.

I entered the Derby as soon as I turned ten. My heart pounded as the day of the race approached. Not far from home, a dirt track intersected the bitumen road and fell away steeply to the bottom of the slope. In dry weather, we challenged each other to drive down and turn sharply without tipping over. Anyone who tipped over, broke his axle or buckled a wheel had to sit with the losers until only one contestant remained.

All too soon, two years passed and my Billy Cart Derby days ended. I began a new life when I entered High School.

Chapter 12

AT THE AGE OF TWELVE I moved from the colonial-style brick primary school, to the prefabricated Portland High School, which was a bit further from home. There, too, many of the teachers seemed indifferent to their vocation, and their writing on the blackboard remained illegible for most of the time. But now I rode to school on my first brand new bicycle—a Malvern Star, 24-inch and bright red.

I washed my bicycle daily and lost track of time when out riding. Tough and durable, my bike took me to places that would have been out of reach on shank's pony. At times, I had to push my bike or lift it over fences and creeks. We were inseparable.

One day when pedalling up-hill I raised myself from my seat and stood to gain momentum. The chain came off and I plummeted head-over-heels onto the handlebars and over the front wheel. I lay there, with the bike on my chest, head spinning, spots before my eyes. Doubled up in agony, I scrambled to my feet. My main concern was the damage I'd done to my precious Malvern Star and wondered whether I'd now speak forever with a funny high-pitched squeaky voice.

I will never forget the excruciating pain. When it lessened, I dragged my bike off the road. Fortunately, it was undamaged, and my voice remained the same, but the gravel rash stung for a long time.

Jim McCracken and I had attended Primary School together, and we now found ourselves in the same class at High School. On school days I'd drop in to my friend's home, then ride to school via the coast. Jim's family radiated joy and his mother always greeted me with a smile that stretched from ear to ear.

Mrs McCracken never let me leave without breakfast. She'd pout her lips and say, 'I'll be very cross with you if you don't have something before you go.'

She clasped her hands to her chest and watched me, while I gulped down my food like a starving puppy. Her large matronly bosom shook with laughter when I thanked her before leaving.

Both the Primary and the High School students shared a football oval, which was out-of-bounds to us except during sports. To prove how defiant we were to authority, we would leave our bikes on the far side, and stride across the oval in all types of weather.

Looking back over the years, I realise what fools we'd been. Fortunately for us, folk were more honest in those days and even though we didn't lock our bicycles, they were never stolen.

After cutting through the football field, we would come across a quiet spot surrounded by a cypress hedge, where vagrants sprawled on bedrolls and talked among themselves. They grasped bottles in brown paper bags and, every so often, take a swig from the bottles. They went to any lengths to hide them, so I used to think they held something of great value.

One day, we heard a bloke singing:

> *Daddy catch fishy*
> *Mummy cook fishy*
> *Daddy eats fishy.*

He repeated the words over and over again in a high-pitched voice and half-chuckled to himself. Thinking he was crazy, we stayed clear of them from then on, fearing we might catch their madness.

Count Your Blessings

The coast road was one of my favourite routes for cycling, because the terrain was level, except for the gentle rise past the Catholic Church and the convent next door. I often stopped at the lighthouse to watch the waves spew on the rocks below. I would sit for hours, gazing at the broad expanse of water and the skyline beyond, while waiting for the crash of every seventh wave. As I sat, I would weave dreams of building a hut like Robinson Crusoe. Perhaps because I'd dreamed of going to sea someday, the clouds formed pictures of boats, ships and ocean liners. The constant sight of ships arriving and departing in the harbour strengthened my longing for the sea.

After resting at the lighthouse, I would ride over the sandstone ridges golden with gorse. At the whaling station, I would lean my bike against a wall and roller-coast down the sheer sandy cliff face. If I slid down too fast, I used my heels as a brake. Then I walked on the sand and the spiky fringe of grass that skirted it.

On my return home, Mum's keen eyes fastened on my sand-dusted trousers. 'If you come home like this again, I'll tan the hide off you,' she said.

At times I'd play in a huge pool that had been built to haul whales in before cutting them up for boiling to extract the blubber. I would climb into a ruined chimney and play within the rusty cauldrons, then ramble over to inspect the remains of an old concrete tank at the summit, pretending it was King Arthur's castle.

My mother's spankings didn't prevent me from wandering among the whalebones littered around the foot of the cliffs, but on my return home, sand was not the only thing implanted on my bottom.

Jim McCracken and I frequently spent weekends together. One fine Saturday morning in spring, Jim rolled up at our front gate in well-creased trousers on his shining new Raleigh. We rode up to the convent, winked at each other, and leaned our bikes against the building. The place held an air of mystery and I often wondered what lay behind the walls because Mum often said, 'Queer things go on inside and if you don't behave yourself, *you'll* be sent there.'

Now, we'd arranged to discover what lay behind the convent walls. With a fluttery stomach and increased heartbeat, I knelt and locked my hands as Jim stepped on them and gawped over the stone parapet. Then he knelt, and did the same for me.

A fine two-storeyed building with wide verandahs towered before us. The garden was not only beautiful but peaceful. A cave with a statue of a lady in a long white dress occupied a prominent position in the front yard. I looked around for any evidence of witchcraft— cauldrons for brewing spells like Macbeth's witches—but saw nothing incriminating.

Curiosity satisfied, we sped off before the nuns saw us and singed our hair with a bolt of lightning.

Only in later years did I discover the identity of the woman in white. It was a statue of the Madonna who had appeared to three children at Lourdes in February 1850.

Jim and I often cycled to the crest of the hill and stood on the railway bridge to watch trains. The earth would tremble as the engine roared past, enveloping us in hot black smoke. We tingled with excitement, wondering whether the bridge would collapse with the vibration.

Coughing and sputtering, we'd get on our bikes and speed past the hospital to a park that had grassy ripples like the swell of an ocean. We rode up and down the undulating area, and little shivers would run down my spine as we rose in the air and landed with a bump.

I nicknamed the place 'The Humps.' Only later did I discover they were furrows made by Edward Henty's plough in 1834, when he had established a settlement, which had started Victoria's agricultural era.

One Saturday morning, during the school holidays Jim sauntered up to our home. He wore a pair of ragged jeans, an old blue jumper and a pair of sneakers, so I knew we were in for a spot of adventure.

'What have you been doing? Haven't seen you around lately,' he said.

I wiped off traces of pastry crumbs from my face. 'Went fishing... Would you like a mulberry pie?'

Jim waved his hands. 'No, thanks. Not this time. We're going to explore the islands. The whole gang's coming.'

I rushed to fetch my bicycle, but Jim stopped me. 'No bikes today. We're going to build a bridge to the heart of the marsh.'

My pulse raced. We'd been planning to do this for some time. I loved building things and couldn't wait. Mum had made dozens of hand-sized pies that morning, so I grabbed a few pies for lunch, filled a bottle with water and followed my friend.

About half a mile from home, just up the road and across from the meat-works, was a swamp covered with little islands of reeds. The water level had fallen due to the dry weather and a soft carpet of dead plants had accumulated during the drought. A good time to build a bridge, I thought.

Robert and Barry Cook sat at the edge of the bog, carving whistles from reeds. When we arrived, they pocketed their penknives and whistles, and started to cut down saplings. A creek divided the town into two halves, and formed a wetland that sank into a golden field of reeds. An old causeway broad enough for a horse to walk on had been constructed of soil, allowing the creek to flow beneath its timber archways during the wet season. The ramp was ideal for cycling at top speed, but this time we ignored it and concentrated on the work in hand.

We laid the reeds down to form a path and jumped over lichened logs. Birds trilled and insects hummed. At our approach, frogs croaked and leapt off the reeds into the water. In some places, reeds blocked our way, so we had to lean forward and press them down before making any headway. Laughing and joking, we balanced like tight-rope artistes over the treacherous areas. Any boy who fell into the muck, would stink of decaying plant matter and became the butt of constant jokes. I took great care not to fall in, and because Mum had warned me to watch out for tiger snakes, I stepped warily, my eyes darting in all directions.

Some time back, I'd come across a brown snake—a Joe Blake coiled up within inches of my feet. I had jumped sideways, as though the Good Lord snapped His fingers, making me land ten feet away. Fortunately for us, even when wading knee-deep through water and crashing among head-high reeds, we never encountered any tigers—I mean tiger snakes, of course.

We pushed our way through to the next island. Our shoes squelched in the mud. The air was rank with the stench of rotting eggs and decaying matter. However, that didn't deter us from having fun. Finally, we came to a grassy knoll and breathed in the delightful perfume of wattle, glad to get away from the humid atmosphere.

Long ago, a farmer had cut a canal through the swamp to a small pond and installed a hand-pump to supply water for his farmhouse. Now a grass-covered mound, the ruins of the building stood, the only link with the past.

I vividly recall the day when a rival gang, waving sticks and yelling, invaded our domain. One of the bigger boys headed for me. Planting both feet firmly on the ground, I grabbed a fallen branch and swung its spiky end like a mace. I could not dodge him because of my special boots, so I remained where I was and braced myself for his attack.

'Come on,' I cried in false bravado.

All hell broke loose. The others were already grappling with each other. Rolling on the ground. Kicking and swearing. All I could do was to show a brave front and point my weapon at my foe in the hope of warding him off. He whooped like a Red Indian and I saw the band of feathers on his forehead. His painted face was fierce and threatening.

My courage failed me. My heart pounded, hammering against my chest, clamouring to get out. I tried to spit to show my contempt but there was nothing there.

The feathered enemy was almost upon me when his foot slipped on the mossy ground and he landed with a thump. He remained there—the breath knocked out of his body. I glanced down at him. He was helpless and at my mercy. Time for revenge.

He rolled over and attempted to rise. His face was covered with mud. Blood poured from his mouth. Unable to fight a fallen foe, I extended a hand to help him to his feet, but the sharpened end of a stick flew towards me like a spear, piercing my skull and tearing off part of my scalp and hair. Like a Roman army, the enemy had placed their reserves in the bushes behind.

My hand flew to my head. I felt no pain at first, but blood streamed down my face and my hand was red and sticky. Blood trickled into my mouth. Blood spattered over my shirt. Blood mingled with the swamp.

No longer capable of being part of the battle, I took one more look at my friends, who appeared to have gained the upper hand. I staggered home, flicking off blood from my face.

'Did you get into a fight?' Mum asked, as soon as I got home.

'Fell off the bike,' I mumbled, hoping she didn't notice I hadn't taken my bike.

She shaved one side of my head, giving me a modern-day Mohawk-style haircut—unheard of back then. The wound took ages to heal.

At the next skirmish, a piece of slate cut the bridge of my nose. I peddled home, half-blinded by the blood that poured down my face.

Mum said, 'You're accident-prone,' and patched me up with a Band-Aid.

The scab fell off, leaving a little dent that I still carry. A relic of boyhood fights.

Another adventure I had with my mates, involved an old deserted house on a slightly elevated area overlooking a section of open water. All life had long fled from the house, and mould covered the structure. My friends said that the place was haunted, but I refused to believe in ghosts. 'Well, not in the day time anyway,' I conceded.

The house, a rugged two-storey building constructed of rocks from the local area, must have been a hundred years old. The owner had plastered the rocks with cement and, apart from the broken window panes, the rest of the residence remained in a sound condition. The doors only partly opened, as if someone objected to our trespassing on its domain.

Before entering we poked our heads in and peered through the gap, our bodies quivering with fear and excitement. The hair on my scalp stirred and I grew cold. I felt someone watching and imagined a presence moving in the shadows.

We waited, breathless...When we had assured ourselves, it was safe to enter, we pushed into the cathedral-like gloom, brushing off cobwebs from our faces.

The spirits of those who had passed away must have watched us pause before we crept in. The hairs on the back of my neck rose as I felt a breath of cold air, but I pressed on. If one of us bolted, the rest would join in the stampede. We paused at the foot of the stairway, and when we'd gathered up all our courage, we tiptoed up the rickety stairs in single file to the attic.

A musty odour greeted us as we entered. Quiet and full of shadows, the attic held on to memories of long ago. Memories, now like dry leaves in the wind.

Later, we explored the back of the house, where the skeleton of a storage shed reared its head. A stone wall kept stock out of the courtyard, where there was a deep stone-lined well. The water disappeared in summer and reappeared like a sprite in winter. We leaned over into the black and forbidding well and shouted, listening to the echoes. Only by dropping a pebble and timing how long it took to hit the water, did we realise how deep it was.

One of the bigger boys cut down the tallest sapling and used it to probe the depths, but he never could reach the bottom.

'It must go all the way down to the earth's core,' I burst out, thinking of Jules Verne's *Journey to the Centre of the Earth*.

'They live down there, so be careful,' an older boy said.

I didn't know to whom he referred, but daren't ask as the fearsome looks of the bigger boys frightened me. Had we remained silent and lingered on, we may have heard the voices of those who dwelt within.

No one ever ventured into that old stone home alone. As the years passed, some of my friends left for boarding school and the gang broke up. The building was battered by wind, rain and storm. Vandals took possession of our old haunt, stripped the roof and ripped off the floorboards. White ants then moved in and destroyed the solid timber beams, leaving only a bare skeleton.

Like so many deserted houses around Portland, it became a shell with only the walls and the long narrow window openings still standing. Stock found their way in and grazed on the grass that now formed a green coffin for the ruins.

The old house remained a place of mystery.

When we left Portland for Canberra, I often wondered about the fate of my old haunts. Years later, I returned with my wife, in search of the ruins. A high school stood not far from the site. My eyes scanned the area. Unable to find any trace of the ruins, I turned to leave but a rusty zinc sheet beneath a pile of rubble, caught my eye. I felt a rush of adrenalin and, using a branch to lever up the metal lid, I uncovered the ancient well. I dropped a pebble into the depths and listened.

'It's still as deep as ever,' I murmured to myself.

My wife stood back, watching me; respecting my need to be alone.

Memories of the past crowded around, submerging my mind in a sea of thoughts. Reluctant to leave, I circled the place, now overgrown with creepers and weeds. A piece of slate lay among the pile of rubble. I picked up the last remnant of my boyhood hangouts.

'This is part of the roof from the haunted house,' I whispered to my wife, as if in a church.

The slate now lies on our mantelpiece—a souvenir of the past.

Chapter 13

WORLD WAR II HAD LEFT many homeless in war-torn countries, so Australia became a target for families searching for peaceful surroundings away from the aftermath of war, because work was plentiful here. In the late forties and early fifties, Portland had a population of about five thousand, but the arrival of migrants, our sleepy village changed forever.

Fred, the Tug-master, a retired English captain who'd seen action during the war, was made Commander of the local Sea Cadets. Dad volunteered for work as his secretary and formed a solid friendship with him, so Fred let me have a look around his tug. One day, he invited Dad to the Royal Trooping of the Colours at HMAS *Cerberus*, a shore-based training ship. What an honour!

Through him, Dad met John Gorton. A rapport grew between them over their drinking sessions, but Dad lost contact with him when Gorton moved to Canberra and became Prime Minister. Later on, we too, left for the nation's capital. We saw John Gorton again, but Dad never attempted to renew his acquaintance with his old drinking mate. I guess that, because of his upbringing, he knew his place and did not wish to embarrass his old drinking buddy.

I joined the local Sea Cadets as soon as I entered High School. In the past, Mum had never let me participate in extracurricular activities like the Boy Scouts, but now she relented. Perhaps she thought it would bring me out of my shell.

The first time Mum saw me in uniform, she clasped me to her.

I squirmed at her sudden show of affection. 'Cor blimey! Cut it out, Mum.'

She released me and wiped her eyes. 'My! How you've grown!'

I practised nautical signals and tied all types of knots. There was rope-splicing, signalling, rifle-drilling and sailing. I learned to climb ropes, to jump over wooden horses, swing on parallel bars, to sling a hammock, steer a ship and make a sail. I rose to the rank of Leading Seaman, visited naval destroyers and proudly stood sentinel on Anzac Day.

Billy Duckworth, a technician with PMG, devoted his time to helping the cadets. He was an excellent leader and drummed into us the necessity of unquestioning obedience. We adored him.

I loved my days as a sea cadet. The sound of water as it slapped against the tug's hull, the creaking of ropes and the sway of the tug, aroused a longing to join the Royal Navy. I forgot my aim of owning a farm, and my one desire now was to matriculate and join the navy.

I studied hard to achieve my goal. Mathematics had been my weakest subject, but at High School I had a good Mathematics teacher who sorted out my problems.

I'll never forget the music teacher, who aroused my interest in classical music. On our first day with her, she asked, 'Has anyone heard of Covent Gardens?'

My hand shot up. Mum and Dad often spoke of the Old Country and had mentioned the name a few times.

'Well,' she said, 'I'm glad *someone* knows.' Her smile reached out to me like a warm embrace. 'I've sung there and have played violin with the London Symphony Orchestra. I'll teach you about famous composers like Mozart and Puccini.'

She was as good as her word and soon taught me to appreciate classical music. From her I learned about composers like Mozart, Bach and Beethoven. She took us to live concerts. I gasped in wonder at the carpeted aisles and dim lights, the hushed sound of voices, the perfume of the ladies and the music from the orchestra. Thrills ran up my spine when I heard the whirr of the curtains as they glided open.

I can't recall my music teacher's name, but it was she who initiated my love of opera. In later years, it led me to frequent opera performances both in Brisbane and in Sydney.

With prosperity in full bloom, money flowed into our house, but like David Copperfield's Micawber, it gushed out faster than it came in. To this day I can never understand why we were always short of cash and why we sometimes found ourselves having to do without a few things like butter and cheese unless Dad brought home some from the docks.

Despite this scarcity of good food at home, Mum began to put on weight and became quite ill in the mornings. The State Savings Bank of Victoria encouraged teachers to open a bank account for each of their pupils and, from the age of six, I'd saved a three-penny bit every week. By the time I reached High School, my savings had swelled to a small fortune. *Perhaps I'll buy my parents exotic gifts when I sail overseas with my ship.*

Before I could reach my goal of joining the navy, as soon as I turned 14, Mum got me to sign the withdrawal form and she withdrew all my savings. It wrenched my heart to see my bank book empty. With it went all my dreams. For days I sported a stony expression and kicked the pebbles that lay on the path in front of our house as if *they* were the obstacle to my life's ambitions.

'You've always wanted to quit school,' my parents said, 'now you're 14 and can legally leave. We think it's a good idea.'

I had not breathed a word of my secret longing to join the Royal Navy, and thinking of our poverty-stricken days, I resolved to persevere in my studies. I had no intention of running short of money when I had my own home.

Little did I think my plans were soon to be crushed.

I never came to know how Mum spent my savings but, on hindsight, she must have spent it on clothes and other items for the baby who was born a few months after that conversation about my leaving school.

Mum raised the subject again, when she returned from hospital. 'Things are not going to be rosy anymore, with an extra mouth to feed,' she said. 'You may continue your studies at a great sacrifice to us, or leave school and find work. Jobs are plentiful. We need the money you'll bring in.'

I'd been the only child for nearly 14 years and found it difficult to adjust to the latest addition to our family. Subconsciously, I rubbed the perspiring palms of my hands up and down my trousers. I was reluctant to leave. I'd grown to like study. Under the circumstances, however, I felt obliged to seek employment so I quit school at the end of the school year.

Some of my friends also went in search of jobs. About the same time, my friend, Derek Knight, commenced his apprenticeship as an electrician. On completion of his studies, he worked with his father repairing fridges. Years later, he opened his own business and prospered.

I was not so fortunate. The end of the school year arrived with the 1960 recession. I applied for a position as a midshipman in the Merchant Navy, but the Shipping Lines rejected my application on the grounds of insufficient education.

When news of my rejection arrived, I hunched my shoulders and wore a bitter smile on my face. I wandered on the beach and threw pebbles into the sea, and watch them sink with all my dreams. I wanted to be alone.

Late that evening, I finally slouched home, both hands in my empty pockets. No words were necessary to convey my feelings. Dad's face crumpled when he saw me.

The next day he urged Fred, the Tug-master, to introduce me to a Greek shipping magnate, who'd registered his tramp steamer under the Panama flag. The ship was to touch in at Asia on its way to Canada.

Fred straight away introduced me to the captain whose leathery face bore the ravages of sun, wind and sea. He showed me my cabin—a tiny room with a bunk. Well, I thought, at least I won't be living with the other seamen in cramped conditions and sleep in a hammock!

Although I had not signed any papers and my passport was not ready, Mum said, 'I'll post your passport out to you when it comes in from Canberra.' Her voice was soft and full of sympathy.

Disappointed by being unable to join the Royal Navy or the Mercantile Navy I said, 'OK. I'll leave home straight away.'

I wanted to show my resentment for having had to leave school, but my voice was shaky.

'You won't be sailing for the next two days,' Mum said, in a pleading voice. 'Why don't you spend your last two nights at home?'

With a great show of reluctance, I obliged her, but I helped clean, scrub, paint and load the craft, thrilled at the thought of going to sea even in a decrepit-looking craft.

On the evening before departure, Fred came to see Dad. He thrust out his lower lip and said, 'Keep him away from the ship.'

From the certainty of his tone, he must have received some inside information about things, but I didn't realise it at the time, so I clenched my fists and stormed back to my room. *I've already left school, and now I'm told I can't go to sea! Why does my life have to change so often? Do I have no control over my own life?*

After a restless night, I eventually fell asleep.

The next morning, I sulked in bed until after the ship's scheduled departure time. I rose late with no desire for breakfast. *What is in store for me now?* All hopes of going to sea dashed aside, I was on the brink of a dark abyss—an absolute void. The future rose before me like a brick wall too high to scale. I pressed my hands to my temples. *If I'd completed my education, I'd have been accepted in the Royal Navy. Now I can't even join this tramp ship!*

Then the radio blared out that the crew had mutinied and set fire to the vessel. Like a duck with a crippled wing unable to fly away, the ship lay in the docks for repairs.

After repairs, the vessel left port without its lawful skipper. I never did find out the cause of the mutiny because Fred remained tight-lipped about the whole affair.

I saw the captain in Portland a few weeks after the ship's departure. He was in civvies and, at first, I failed to recognise him, but as he drew closer, I knew him straight away. He wore a grey suit and looked careworn. A strand of white hair escaped from his hat, increasing the impression of weariness. He must have been too engrossed in his own thoughts to notice me.

Looking back over the years, I thank God for my narrow escape. *What would have happened to me had I joined the ship and gone to sea as planned? What would have happened if I was on board when the crew mutinied?*

If the crew hadn't mutinied, I'd have been smuggled into the vessel and been an illegal passenger until my passport arrived. If my passport failed to reach me, I could never return to Australia.

Despite my love of the sea and the magic of the unknown, I eventually resigned myself to doing odd jobs for farmers and helping them dip sheep in coloured chemicals.

In spring, when foot rot spread among the herd, I'd scrape off the black rotten flesh from affected animals, using a sharp knife and digging down until I reached healthy tissue. If not treated early, the crippled sheep would hobble around on their knees and the farmer had no alternative but to shoot the lame ones. The odour of their putrid feet made my breakfast rise to my throat but I persevered in my work, hoping to alleviate their pain.

Their cries of distress wrung my heart, reminding me of my own distress at not going to sea.

The most cruel but fascinating work for me was castrating the animals. Farm hands taught me how to place a rubber ring tightly around a sheep's testicles. The sheep kicked and bleated at first, but they grew quiet when numbness replaced the pain. Soon the testicles withered and died from lack of blood.

As the year passed, I clung on to my sea-going dreams. I longed to own a boat—a fourteen-footer, but I could only afford a ten-footer. Seeing an advertisement in a magazine for one in kit form, I sent a cheque for ninety-five pounds to the Melbourne shipyards. Dad arranged for a local truckie to bring the bits and pieces, free of charge, from Melbourne.

The kit arrived with a fully constructed hull.

After weeks of work, Dad and I finished the seats and gunwales. I painted my boat a bright red, using the best anti-foul paint—the kind used on the fishing fleet. As soon as I earned sufficient money, I put in an order for the oars.

I never gave the little craft a proper name, although everyone made various suggestions.

Mum said, 'Call your boat *The Little Emily* like Steerforth in *David Copperfield.*'

Dad shook his head. 'Call her *The Albatross.*'

I had no wish to name my boat after a girl and felt inclined to dad's choice, but unwilling to offend either of my parents, I called it 'The Boat.'

Dad fitted the old box trailer with two pieces of four-by-two lengths of timber to form a 'V' at each end. We drove to the beach, lifted the vessel into the sea and, with a heart thumping so hard it felt ready to burst at any moment, I set off to explore the harbour.

The cost of a permanent mooring was prohibitive, so Dad would tow it to and from the port. At times, we'd catch cold-water salmon weighing two to three pounds. Our muscles ached, but we held on, struggling with our huge catch.

We used hemp lines. 'They're better than the plastic, nylon stuff,' Dad said.

Once, a migrating whale decided to do a back flip. Waves rocked the up and down, sending thrills down my spine. It was wonderful!

Early one Sunday morning, we decided to anchor on a reef outside the harbour, within a mile or so of the cliffs. The weather was calm, so we decided to take our chance. The fishing was good and absorbed all our attention.

Our small boat had an anchor of sorts—an old steel wheel from a broken barrow, which was useless in deep water or during rough weather. While we were preoccupied with the fishing, our makeshift anchor relinquished its hold on the reef and dangled helplessly. The boat drifted out to sea.

Only when the sea turned choppy and drenched us with spray did we realise our plight. Hearts pumping, we pulled for home. During stormy weather, large vessels would shelter in the bay behind the rocky headland because even they were not immune to its fury. What would have been an easy one-mile row out in calm water was now like a four-mile tussle in rough seas that ran against us. The plywood-bottom bent inwards with each crash. Dad sat in the bow and hung on to the sides until his knuckles went white. He groaned whenever we hit a wave. His face turned green. Fortunately, he didn't get seasick or I'd have been drenched, not merely by the waves but by the contents of his stomach.

I made for the breakwater. Once around the point, we could swim to the rocks if the vessel capsized. I worked hard at the oars with blistered hands for what seemed hours. My muscles heaved and my lungs felt like bursting. My heart spasmed. My shoulders shuddered. My emotions surged and rose to the surface. *Will we ever reach shelter? What will Mum do if we don't return this evening and our bodies drift back to shore?*

Knowing the strength of the ocean, I expected our tiny craft to splinter into smithereens. Waves tossed 'The Boat,' but she held on. The heads of people on shore loomed and receded from view as the boat surged and dipped. We drew closer to land.

Two long hours later, we were in calm water and only a short easy row from where we had left the car. Dad never came out fishing or took the boat down after that but, despite the danger, the thrill of adventure never stopped me from venturing into deep water with my boat. Neither of us told Mum about our near-drowning experience, so I asked her to tow me to the harbour whenever Dad was on night-shifts at the docks.

Mum loved garfish. A friend possessed a net, but had no boat, so she rounded up twenty men, promising them a share in the spoils if they pitched in to help. I went out with two men and cast the net, spreading it out for several yards.

We took turns to row up and down the shoreline, dragging the nets after us. The others waited on the beach until we came in. Then they waded into the water and hauled in the nets that took our combined strength to bring in the load of fish.

Once home, Mum rewarded me with a meal of garfish garnished with parsley.

This clandestine fishing continued whenever Dad worked at the docks.

One evening the local police officer happened to pass. 'Hope you're using a regulation-size net.' He probably suspected us of catching undersized gar.

'Of course,' Mum replied. 'Have a look at the net when the men return after dark.' She handed him something wrapped in newspaper. 'Like some garfish for supper?'

'Oh yes.' He looked around and then put his hand out and took the fish. 'It'll be too late for me to wait until their return.' A twinkle was in his eyes, but his face remained serious.

That was the way with country cops in those days.

Chapter 14

DURING THE FIFTIES, PORTLAND boasted of having the only deep water-harbour between Adelaide and Melbourne. Wool, wheat and frozen meat were exported from the hinterland and the town waxed fat in wealth. Despite the town's growth, the Wool Complex that Dad had built closed in 1959 and business shifted to Geelong. The ears of the politician responsible for the move must have been burnt right off by the way the people of Portland talked about him. Their grumbling failed to save Portland, however, because all went into a downward spiral and the town went from boom to bust.

The recession of the 1950s continued into the 1960s, forcing people to leave for greener pastures. My parents couldn't afford the rent for our cottage by the sea, and to make matters worse, our car kept breaking down, so we moved to our block of land in Portland.

Dad slaved from dawn to dusk, using second-hand materials to build our home. The Council condemned the building, but he refused to quit the premises.

I wore old castoff clothes and remained jobless for weeks. By the time my fifteenth birthday arrived, I'd found work as an assistant to a professional rabbit trapper. My heart sang with joy because I had found a job after being unemployed for so long.

Count Your Blessings

My boss owned a thousand traps, an old station wagon and a spade. Each morning he'd pick me up from home and park his car in a shady spot, then trudge for miles across paddocks, heading for a rabbit-proof fence. Once there we looked for rabbit tracks and set the snares.

At the end of the day, we emptied and reset the traps to capture rabbits that frisked about from dusk to dawn. At times, the trap only held a hind leg because the poor creature had kept on tugging until the iron teeth stripped its flesh and tore off a limb. If the rabbit's foreleg was caught, the bone broke, leaving the animal in agony until we ended its misery. Pain rose in my throat. I wished there was a more humane way to catch rabbits but there was nothing I could do about it.

The trapper taught me to look for signs of myxomatosis such as swelling of eyelids, ears, face and genitalia. Any discharge from the eyes and ears also meant that dread disease. Myxomatosis had been introduced to Australia in 1950 as a biological control agent for rabbits which had spread to plague proportions. We killed the rabbits that showed any sign of the disease and left them in the bush to rot.

We collected a total of about eight hundred healthy rabbits daily, carried the carcasses to a central area and gutted them. Then we cut a hole in their hind legs and threaded a string through it. I tied them in pairs and slung the rabbits across a pole I carried over my shoulder. To keep the blowflies off, I covered the bodies with a hessian bag. Blood trickled over me, staining my clothes as I walked. My shirt grew stiff with it and attracted even more flies. The smell nauseated me, but I kept going until we reached the collection point. From there the carcasses were taken to Melbourne.

Despite the smell, the blowflies and the discomfort, I enjoyed my days in the bush and considered the work as an adventure. We continued trapping rabbits for eighteen months but when landowners ploughed up burrows and placed poisoned baits in the area, the rabbit population diminished so rapidly from myxomatosis that rabbit-trapping was no longer profitable.

My employer gave me some traps before he gave up the business. I would keep one of the rabbits for Mum and sell the rest to local butchers as 'underground mutton'. Times were hard and people bought the rabbits for meat.

I earned only a few shillings and had plenty of time on my hands so, not wishing to remain idle, I borrowed Mum's knitting machine and made beanies. Nearly everyone I knew in Portland bought one, and I soon ran out of customers. Dad's hours of work decreased too. At times, all he had was a few night shifts as a wharfie. The future held out chilly arms for me.

Mum sent me out in search of work. 'Just go and ask,' she said, giving me a nudge.

Cap in hand, I trudged from door-to-door, asking for jobs. Sometimes, I weeded old Jenkins's garden, or helped tidy a warehouse for a day's wages. I could only afford a slim sausage for lunch.

The die-hards continued to remain in Portland. Most people put their property on the market and left. Real estate agents prospered by buying houses well below their value.

My parents hung on, hoping for things to bounce back.

In 1956, when the Olympic Games were held in Melbourne, the state capitals of Sydney and Melbourne were the only two cities to get TV in time to view the event. Later, when television came to Portland, those who could afford it purchased a set and put up aerials to pick up the signals. The rest of us watched TV through shop windows. The black and white pictures were indistinct and looked like falling snowflakes.

With the event of television, I found work helping install aerials. Dad earned twenty-five dollars at the time, and although my wages were low in comparison to his, I was delighted.

I whistled as I raced home. 'I'll be earning four dollars a week, Mum,' I said.

She reached out and tousled my hair.

My job was to hold a thirty-foot length of timber upright, while the boss bolted it to the building. I attached the aerials either to the back to the house, fence, or even on a star picket and pushed up a length of water pipe with the end of the aerial tied to it. The boss, who sat in a bosun's chair, suspended by guy ropes, then secured it to the top of the timber. A rope held him about sixty feet above. I hoped and prayed the rope didn't break and bring him down on top of me.

With the construction of relay stations, people no longer needed such high aerials and I was again left jobless. Within a few months, the upper sections of the aerials bent downwards, paying homage to the strong southerly winds.

Harold, a part-time farmer, employed me to plant potatoes or do odd jobs on his farm. His father owned a property but spent his days at the pub, leaving his wife and sons to do the work.

'All he ever does is to plough his Fourex at the Max Hotel,' Dad used to say.

Harold's mother laid on a hearty meal for lunch. Her bowl of hot soup, roast lamb and vegetables spread warmth through my body. I ate the treacle pudding slowly, allowing the taste and texture to linger on, before gulping down the coffee.

Rubbing my stomach in satisfaction, I'd pour out my thanks and dash back to work.

Harold and I worked for other farmers on weekends.

Harold had a brother who rarely spoke. No one knew his name and everyone ignored him except to say, 'Give us a hand, will you?'

One day, the two brothers signed a contract to plant two acres of a farmer's property with potatoes. They supplied the seed, the superphosphate and labour. The farmer agreed to do the ploughing and give each of us part of his crop as payment.

We drove through a long dirt track to a farm in the middle of the bush. The farmer ploughed a furrow, and the two brothers loped along laying spuds. I followed, putting in a handful of superphosphate for each spud.

The farmer continually found fault with us. Waving his fist, he'd shout, 'You've planted the potatoes incorrectly—the eyes are not facing up.'

Another time he'd say, 'Colin, you didn't spread the fertiliser correctly.'

One day, he stopped the tractor beneath a gum tree and just sat there. We waited for him to plough the next row. Minutes passed.

'Time for our break,' Harold said. He poured out three mugs of tea from a flask and sat down.

The farmer continued to remain motionless.

After a short time, Harold put down his mug. 'What's the old fool doing?'

'Nothing.' His brother's shoulders nearly reached his ears as he shrugged.

'He's switched off the motor,' I said. 'Should I go over and find out why he's not joining us?'

Harold patted the tree trunk. 'Sit down.'

He finished his tea before striding over. We followed.

The farmer continued to sit motionless.

Harold wiped his mouth with his sleeve. 'Perhaps he's fallen asleep.' He went over and put his hand upon his shoulder. 'What's up, mate?'

I thought the old man was dead, and expected him to fall off his tractor, but he opened his eyes and glanced at his watch. 'Ah ten minutes. Everything's all right.'

'What's all right?'

'I ran over a tiger and it sprang on me.' He touched a spot of dried blood on his neck.

'Why didn't you say something? Why just sit and do nothing?'

'I waited because, if the tiger had bitten me, I'd die before getting to the hospital.'

Harold returned to the utility and got out his shotgun. We converged on the tree in search of the snake, moving fallen branches and rusty old sheets of metal. Perspiration ran down our backs and our shirts clung to our bodies.

Nothing showed up. The farmer had made us waste so much time and there was no trace of the snake. Harold trembled with rage and looked as though he wanted to shoot the old man.

No one moved. Our breathing became faster and louder. *Is he really going to shoot the farmer?*

A flock of crows landed on the branches, distracting Harold. He swung around and, raising his gun, let off two barrels in their midst. The birds flew off unharmed, but the ricochet peppered down on us. My skin stung for hours.

Harold then turned on his brother and swore the foulest oaths I'd ever heard. His brother retaliated. He had never before uttered a word, but now Harold must have goaded him into fighting back. His words spilled out like a torrent. I guess the tension of having to support their parents and unmarried sister during a recession finally broke them.

The two only stopped quarrelling when the sun dipped behind the gum trees.

We returned to the utility in silence. Dog-tired, I must have dozed off a dozen times. When we reached home, Harold gave me a gentle kick on my backside.

His brother had vanished. I never saw him again. Neither did I receive a single potato in payment for the day's labour.

I worked with Harold many times after that incident. His father continued to spend his days drinking at the Max Hotel while his family ran the farm. He had a daughter who entered a novitiate in Melbourne.

When I first went to work with Harold, Mum warned, 'Don't you ever speak to him about his sister.'

It sounded as though the girl was undergoing a jail sentence—something to be ashamed of.

Mum was prejudiced against the Catholic Church, but her words made me wonder what wrong the poor thing had done.

Harold had paid a sum of money for her dowry as his father wouldn't give her a penny.

Within a year, Harold's sister decided that life in a convent was too rigid for her, and returned home. The nuns gave her back her dowry so that she could start life afresh.

When the news reached Mum, she passed on the gossip to me, a triumphant look in her eyes.

'She couldn't have committed such a grave offence if she came back so soon,' I said, thinking a novitiate was a prison for young women.

Mum just glared at me.

When Harold didn't need me, I hung around with a man named Mr Dent, who worked with Dad on the boats. He was the youngest of twelve boys, and was called Axi. He told Dad that he was an unplanned addition to the family; hence, his name, Axi Dent.

Axi found me a job with Rob, a labourer who worked on the town's main water supply pipes.

'He's a bit of a crook,' Dad warned me. 'Watch him.'

Rob often spent Saturday nights in the lock-up for being drunk and disorderly. The sergeant would let him out on Sunday morning after he'd chopped wood for the station's kitchen stove. He smoked like a chimney and drank like the proverbial fish, but I found him rather amusing.

At the end of the day's work, Rob would ask me look out for his vehicle.

'What colour is the car? I asked.

'You can't miss it. Single door coupe. Bright red—and there'll be a gorgeous blonde—my girlfriend—driving it. Just wave out and she'll stop and pick me up.'

Funny thing though, I never did get to see either his car or his girl. Only later did I realise how gullible I'd been.

That was the least of his faults. At times, Rob worked for a local carter who ran a fleet of trucks between Melbourne and Portland.

One day, his employer told Rob to drive a truck to Melbourne and pick up a load of chain saws. 'In case of discovery, you must agree to take the blame for the theft in return for a bonus to keep your trap shut.'

The police picked Rob up a few days after he'd delivered the stolen goods, and his employer paid a sum of money for Rob's wife during his time in jail.

Rob sat with downcast eyes in the courtroom until the judge

appeared. Then he blurted out, 'I plead Queen's evidence.'

He testified against his employer and got off unscathed. Harold kept the bonus and did a moonlight-flit while his boss served time in prison.

Dad had a see-what-I-told-you-look on his face when we came to hear of it.

By then, I'd turned seventeen, and labouring was the only job open to me. I received a third of an adult's wage, even though I had to carry the same weight as the men.

The strain on my back caused problems later in life because my discs wore out and some of the fluid oozed out. Years later, it solidified and caused agony whenever it touched a nerve.

Months passed. I finally obtained a position as a telegraph-messenger boy in the Post Office and was given a bike for work. I thought of Shakespeare's immortal words, 'All's well that ends well,' and felt like a million dollars.

The Post Master frequently said, 'You're an industrious and cheerful worker. If you continue in this manner, you'll soon rise to be a postman and end up as postmaster.'

The recession had been a difficult time. I had struggled to search for the silver lining, and here it was now. I felt warm inside, and the thought of having a steady job cheered me. It was the best job I'd ever had so far. A shining future appeared to lie ahead of me. I could start saving to buy a farm and have cows like Pa Newton.

Chapter 15

ONE MORNING, DAD SAW AN advertisement for bricklayers, offering good wages with three months' free board and lodging in Canberra. The building firm promised an immediate start, so he departed straight away. Dad left us to arrange for the move to the national capital, while he looked for a suitable house for us. He would no longer have to struggle to support us.

Mum sold the house and land. On our last day in Portland, I rode my bike to all my childhood haunts. On my journey of nostalgia, I visited the islands where we had so many adventures. I lingered on at the haunted house, slunk home and collapsed into a chair. *Things had been looking so bright for me. Why do I have to leave Portland? Why do I have to leave the Post Office? Why do I have to give up everything? My hopes and dreams and job?*

At dinner, I said, 'Why can't I remain in Portland? I could board with Mr and Mrs Cooke.'

Mum put down her spoon and fork. She glared at me. 'Because you're old enough to help your Dad. We've spent all these years bringing you up and paying for your education. It's *your* turn to do something.'

I rarely argued with my mother, but anger and desperation gave me courage. 'Education? What education? You took me out of school as soon as I turned fourteen. Now you want me to leave a good job and come to Canberra!'

'Yes. We have an extra mouth to feed and it's your duty to do something for the family.'

'Excuse me.' The words choked in my throat. Sick to the core, I left the room and threw myself on my bed.

It had always been like this. If any sacrifice was needed, I was the one who had to give up my desires.

But I'd been brought up to obey, and I did just that.

Because we could only take what fitted into our car and box-trailer, Mum asked friends and neighbours whether they'd like to buy our furniture and other non-essential items.

When packing, I missed my Meccano set and my cricket bat. *Mum usually lets me pack my own things. Where are they?*

'I can't find my Meccano set or cricket bat anywhere, Mum,' I said. 'Did you put them in the trailer?'

'No, son', she said. 'Cookie wanted them for his boys and offered me a good price.'

I could scarcely believe my ears. 'You don't mean to say you took *my* things and sold them off? Dad bought me the bat and you and Dad gave me the set as a birthday gift.'

'You're too old to play with toys, and you won't have time for cricket when you're working. You're fortunate I left you your rifle. Cookie wanted that too.'

I sprang from my chair. *This is too much. Even before Sally was born, I had to sacrifice school. Now here she is. Sitting on her mother's lap and sucking on an icy pole! As a child, I had to wait for Christmas, Easter, or my birthday before they bought me an ice cream!*

Sally had already vandalised my encyclopaedia, so *that* couldn't be sold. Mum had allowed her to draw on my books and our photo albums, and she had cut out pictures from them and destroyed our cherished family photos.

Nearly three now, she was adored by both parents, who gave in to her slightest whims as she invariably had a tantrum if denied anything.

'Leave your sister alone,' they'd say, whenever I tried to remonstrate against such behaviour.

'Spare the rod, spoil the child,' had been their motto until she was born. I'd received a strict upbringing, but Mum, being the only girl among a family of four boys, longed to have a daughter. A gypsy fortune-teller in England had predicted she'd have a female child who'd cause her heartaches.

Mum had chuckled. 'Gypsies are always trying to shock people, hoping they'll be back for more readings.'

In the end, the fortune-teller's story came to pass. Mum did shed many tears over Sally.

As soon as I realised that I'd never see my Meccano set and cricket bat again, I packed whatever little of mine remained, and stayed in my room until breakfast.

We left Portland in November 1962. Mum and I took turns to drive, even though I was not old enough to obtain a driver's licence. We only had short comfort stops and breaks for meals. Sally slept most of the time and I dozed off whenever Mum took over the wheel.

It was late when we arrived at our new house in Bursaria Street, Canberra. With winter fast approaching, evening had crept in early. I got out from the car. A mournful wind broke the stillness. The outline of the building was lost in the gathering darkness—the moon obscured by

Count Your Blessings

a blanket of cloud. Ghost gums dripped dew and deepened the gloom. Our golden retriever leapt out. She sank back on her hind legs, shivering. Then she pointed her nose skyward and howled.

I heard someone running down the stairs and Dad stepped out from the shadows. Goldie leapt at him and licked his face but she refused to follow us indoors.

I shrugged my shoulders and joined my parents.

Mum went from room to room, showing us where to put things. 'You made a good choice,' she said, turning to Dad.

She walked to the back bedroom. 'Why is this locked?'

Dad shrugged. 'The previous tenants left without a trace so the owner stored all their belongings here. He says he'll keep them until they pay their arrears of rent. He doesn't charge us much, and we don't need four bedrooms, anyway.'

'It's a lovely house,' Mum agreed. 'Quite modern too, with hot water and even a bath.' She looked longingly at the bath tub as if she wanted to step in right away.

Once we had set down our things and eaten a hurried dinner, Mum, Dad and Sally threw themselves, exhausted, in their beds. As Goldie had refused to come into the house, I laid an empty tea chest on its side and put in a blanket for her. Then I went to my room and settled down to sleep.

Around midnight, footsteps along the corridor woke me. A shadow glided past. *Probably Mum checking on Sally.* I turned over and slept.

The next day, we helped Mum move the furniture around. I found a glass vase in a cupboard and Mum gathered roses from the garden.

'How lovely,' she said, beaming at us. 'Wonder why the tenants quit in such a hurry.'

'Probably did a moonlight flit.' Dad's spirits were high. With good wages and a beautiful house, what more did he want?

Count Your Blessings

That night the wind howled and the temperature dropped several degrees. I tossed and turned in bed. Sally shrieked. She tended to walk in her sleep and have nightmares, so I took no notice and pulled the blanket over my head to smother the sounds. The last thing I heard before dropping off was our retriever whining downstairs.

Next morning at breakfast, Mum asked, 'Did you hear any noises last night, Colin?'

I stretched and gave a slight yawn. 'Yes. Was Sally having a nightmare again?' My sister was only three, but she had a room of her own.

Mum's voice rose. 'Sally came into our room, screaming. I switched on the light and asked if she had a bad dream.

She said, "A man is in my room."

'Your Dad took off like a shot. No one was there. He checked the windows and doors, then came back and sat on the bed.'

Mum's face was white as she related the events to me. 'Sally says he came last night too, but she thought he was one of us. We hadn't been to her that night,' she went on, 'It must have been a prowler! We took Sally back to her room and made a show of searching under the bed and checking the cupboards.'

'You've been dreaming,' I said, putting on a smile to calm her.

'Sally stamped her foot and screamed. "No, it wasn't." I made some hot cocoa for her. She slept with us for the rest of the night.'

On hearing Mum's story, I shrugged. 'I thought she was having a nightmare. She's always having bad dreams. And she *did* tuck into a large meal last night.'

Mum's brow darkened into a frown. 'What if he was going to harm her?'

That frown would have made me shrink into myself in the past, but now I stood my ground. 'If there'd been the sound of a scuffle, of course I'd have gone to help Dad.'

Dad shook his head. Obviously, he also considered the matter serious.

I nodded to indicate I'd be more vigilant in future. *I wouldn't hesitate to protect my sister from danger but there was no need to cater to all her whims and fancies like they did.*

Four nights later, footsteps once again sounded along the hallway towards Sally's room. I leapt from my bed. My parents rushed down the passage. Dad and I overtook Mum and reached the room first.

Sally slept, blonde tresses spread across the pillow, one hand thrown over her head, an angelic smile playing on her lips. No one else was there.

A milky white patch lay on the polished floor.

'Sally must have been sick,' Mum said.

'She had a glass of hot milk for supper,' Dad said.

Mum gazed at the mess on the floor. 'We should have heard her footsteps. But why didn't she call me?' Dark rings showed beneath her eyes.

'Perhaps she was half asleep and vomited the rest in the toilet bowl,' I suggested.

Dad flung open Sally's bedroom window and peered outside. The moon shone brightly and a eucalyptus tree cast its shadow into the room. A cold wind blew. A branch tapped at the window pane.

'That's what we've been hearing! I'll hack the bloody thing off tomorrow.' The muscles in Dad's jaw worked up and down as he glowered at the tree.

I ran my hand through my hair and sighed with relief. *We've solved the mystery. No more restless nights from now on.*

Weeks passed. Then one windy moonlit night I awoke to the sound of approaching footsteps. I lay listening, every muscle tensed. With hollow regularity, the steps moved towards my sister's bedroom. A cold shiver ran down my spine. Although only sixteen, I was tall and sinewy—strong enough to tackle the intruder. I crept out of bed.

Rewarded by a fleeting glance of a shadow, I stalked the predator, ready to pounce and hold him fast until Dad arrived. I followed the man into Sally's bedroom. A cold draft of air blew in and a chill descended over me like a cloud. The fine hairs on my arms bristled. A creeping sensation ran along my spine.

A figure leaned over Sally's bed. I stepped forward to grab him. The apparition turned and glided towards me. I froze—unable to hold it or stop its progress. It walked straight toward me and through me, as if my body was nothing but thin air! I shuddered, recalling my uncanny experience as a child in an abandoned farmhouse. *The unwanted visitor was no mere mortal.*

Later that day, I told Dad what I'd seen, but failed to mention his mysterious disappearance, fearing he'd scoff at me.

'The footsteps always start at the rear bedroom and continue towards Sally's room,' Dad said. 'We'll check what's stored in there.'

While Sally was having her afternoon nap, the three of us crept into the back room. Dad braced himself against me and kicked the door. It groaned open, emitting a musty odour. Mum raced to the window and struggled with the latch. I took over from her and flung it open. A rat raced out from a corner. Mum shrieked.

Fortunately, Sally remained asleep through all the noise we were making.

Mum opened a set of drawers. 'Look at this.' She waved a little frock in the air. 'There are a whole lot of dresses here for a child about Sally's age.' She rummaged around.

After a few minutes, she held up a neatly tied bundle of BHP Share Certificates. 'Why did they leave without their valuables?'

Dad's eyes widened and a vein in his neck throbbed. 'I *said* he'd done a moonlight flit!'

The mystery of the evasive spectre continued. Dad had his evening meal soon after he returned from work and rested in bed until we retired for the night. Then he got up, switched off the lights and waited for the sound of footsteps. He used a different room every night.

Each night, once the sun had sunk behind the horizon and the stars shone outside, footsteps echoed through the house. Not the mere creaking of floorboards or the faint rustling of wind, but clear and measured footfalls—in the hallway, lounge room or kitchen—away from where Dad kept vigil in the silent gloom.

The sound always faded into the shadows, as if the spirit shied away from my dad. I slept with my loaded gun beside my bed. *You can't kill a ghost but the noise may drive off the phantom.*

In the mornings at breakfast, Dad's haggard appearance tore my heart. 'Let me help you, Dad. You can't go on like this without something snapping.' I smiled to soften my words. He didn't take kindly to sympathy.

He shook his head. 'No, no. This is my job. I'll get the bastard even if I have to wait up forever.' He placed his hands on the table and pushed himself up before dragging himself off to work.

Meanwhile, I'd joined a team of workers, who were building an extension on the University of Science and Technology. Within a few months, I obtained an apprenticeship in bricklaying.

Dad bought a block of land in the suburb of Hall, on the outskirts of Canberra, and I put my skills to use, helping construct a solid brick home.

Winter turned to spring and passed on to the scorching heat of summer. We spent Christmas at the haunted house. The wind moaned, the ominous footsteps never stopped nor was the intruder ever caught.

By autumn, Dad could endure no more. 'Our house is now ready. We're moving out. I want to smash his face in, but I can't catch the bastard.'

'You'll never get rid of him,' I said, unable to contain my thoughts any longer. 'He's not human. He needs to be exorcised.'

The idea of getting a priest to exorcise the apparition never occurred to my parents. Neither Dad nor Mum practised any religion although I had attended Sunday school at Portland.

His face creased into a smile. 'He certainly does a lot of nocturnal *exercise.*'

I hadn't seen him smile for months. The decision to leave must have lifted a weight off his shoulders.

The next day, we packed our things and I helped carry them to the trailer. Goldie pranced about, wagging her tail in delight.

We pulled out of the driveway at 3 pm on Good Friday. No birds sang, and except for the spluttering of the vehicle in the drive, silence prevailed. Sally was in front between Dad and Mum. I sat in the back with Goldie. Dad put his foot on the accelerator and drove off, looking straight ahead, but I turned to gaze once more at the haunted house. We had spent a little more than a year in the ghostly premises.

Dark clouds hid the sun. The ghostly gum tree held up the stump of its branch like a maimed arm and shook it as if in reproach. I glanced up at Sally's bedroom. The curtains were drawn. Behind them the silhouette of a man stood, watching us depart.

The wandering spirit, unlike the classic tale of *The Lady in White* by Wilkie Collins, failed to follow us to our new home.

A few months' later, I visited the landlord, told him of our unearthly experience, and asked, 'Why did your tenants leave?'

He gazed into the distance before answering. 'They took off without saying a word and never turned up to claim their belongings. Few tenants remain for long. Some complained of shrieks and strange sightings. You're the only one who has actually seen the spirit. I work on the Snowy Mountain Scheme and stay in the sleepout now, on my days off. I've never caught sight of the intruder. I'm thinking of selling the house and moving out.'

Eight years later, when I married, I took my wife to show her the house we'd stayed in. The building had a desolate, uninhabited air. The neglected rose bushes had gone wild. Thorny branches spread over the path and across the front door. I shuddered and drove off.

Did the little girl who lived there formerly have an untimely death? And did the father's spirit return in search of his daughter? It's impossible to know.

This supernatural experience of ours continued to remain a mystery, but it led to my discovering some of the darkest years of dad's life.

Chapter 16

PERHAPS IT WAS HIS BRUSH with the supernatural that caused Dad to mention his encounter with death. One evening, Dad lit his pipe and settled down with a beer. 'Once, when we were deployed to France, during the war, the sergeant ordered us to bivouac and find our own accommodation. Tired and hungry, a mate and I found a barn next to a cemetery on the outskirts of a bomb-devastated village. The night was pitch-black and already the place was occupied by many others. Reluctant to awaken them, we squeezed in among the sleeping men.

'At reveille, the sun peeped through the trees,' Dad continued. 'We sprang to action, but our companions lay still. Their glazed eyes were blind to the shrapnel-scarred branches and deaf to the twittering of birds. The hair at the nape of my neck rose. I knew they'd never rise again until Judgement Day,' Dad said. 'We hadn't realised that the barn was serving as a temporary mortuary. I can usually sleep anywhere, but not beside the dead. We grabbed our belongings and beat a hasty retreat.'

I remained silent, not wishing to disturb Dad's train of thought.

'In May 1942, I had enlisted in the army and trained as a gunner in Wales,' he said, after a brief pause. 'I nearly died when a gun misfired.'

'Were you wounded?' I didn't recall seeing a scar on his body.

'No, but a sergeant and two others were killed. I awoke in hospital with my head in a bandage. A nurse said a piece of shrapnel had grazed me here.' He lifted his hair and pointed to a small triangle on his forehead.

'Were you out of action for long? Did you get headaches?'

Dad shook his head. 'Soon after my discharge from hospital, I had to report to the regiment and complete my training as a gunner. A few months later, I married your mother, whom I'd been courting for several months.'

I thought of the bloody war movies I'd seen, and shuddered. 'Did you marry during the war?'

'Yes. In September 1942.'

Dad went on to reveal that when he re-joined his unit, the regiment was ordered to sail for Southend, and proceed on to the Zuider Zee as part of a convoy. He had advanced with the forward units, moving on to France sometime in 1944. I realised Dad was confiding in me because he considered me a grown man. *Will he now speak to me about the birds and the bees?*

Dad did not speak to me of the birds and the bees, but Mum tried to arouse my interest in the opposite sex. Busy with work and study, I had never bothered about girls or desired their company. Girls, like my sister Sally, with their constant chatter and demands for attention, would only hinder the pursuit of my goal. I learned to make my heart a sanctuary and withdrew in solitude to the bush. Always cautious, I moored my solitary ship with two anchors.

'I've arranged for you to take my friend's daughter out to a drive-in,' Mum said, one day.

My body tensed. I glared at her. *Why does she always interfere with my life?*

'You're not showing any interest in girls. People may begin to think you're queer!' she said.

I raised my brows and crossed my arms. 'Let them think what they like. I'm happy as I am.'

'You're spending too much time hanging out with your mates. What's this about getting a quote for a racing car?'

'A *rally* car,' I said. 'Canberra has the right terrain for rally-driving.'

'About time you looked around for a decent girl,' Mum said.

'What's your idea of a decent girl?'

'That's for you to find out. Just take her out to a drive-in and everything will fall into place. You're not committing yourself to marry her.'

I invariably try to avoid an argument, especially with Mum. 'All right. You win. Don't ever do that again or I'll search for lodgings elsewhere.' I clamped my lips shut.

Mum smiled triumphantly. She knew she'd won.

I soon discovered that my date was as bashful as I was. She had a fine figure that aroused me but I wasn't going to be dictated to by my mother. When I'd completed my studies and the time was ripe, I'd choose a girl who suited me. But not just yet.

My date wore a pale shade of lipstick and a matching nail polish. Her hair was held up by a bow, which was in fashion at the time. The swinging knee-high skirt revealed her knees invitingly. I was torn between running my fingers through her long silky hair or placing my hand upon her knee, but she sat as close as possible to the window, leaving a space between us. My eyes lingered on her well-filled blouse, trimmed with lace. I don't usually notice what a woman wears, but here I was, alone in the car with a girl on a cold winter's evening.

'I love winter,' I said, trying to make small talk.

She nodded.

'Is it too cold for an ice cream?' I asked before the movie started.

She shook her head.

'Hang on a minute. I'll get something for us to munch on.'

The girl nodded and I left, glad for an excuse to escape for a few minutes. I returned with two ice cream cones and two packets of chips.

'Thanks.' She started on the ice cream.

We sat in silence, licking our cones. When the film commenced, the only sound was the crinkle of the packet of chips as she opened it. I, too, began chomping on mine. I'd chosen *Lawrence of Arabia* as my mates had been speaking of the movie with enthusiasm.

I was soon lost in the film, but at times, the girl beside me seemed to deliberately distract me.

After eating, she crushed the paper, wrapped it in a tissue and slipped it into her handbag. She kept twisting her scent-soaked handkerchief in her hands, sending a strong fragrance towards me. My nostrils twitched. I shifted in my seat and suppressed a sneeze. Then I rubbed my nose to stop the tickling sensation. I imagined that the girl expected me to snuggle up to her, but I longed to breathe in the chemical-free atmosphere. *If only I could get a whiff of pure air!*

The night was cold and the warmth of the heater in the car prevented me from letting in the icy night air.

'Good, and cuddly weather,' my friends had said, when I'd told them I'd be taking a girl to the drive-in.

I wished it were a hot, summer's night so I had an excuse to open the window and get a life-saving draught of oxygen. I berated myself for choosing such a long film. It was one I'd have enjoyed watching with my mates but I don't think I'd made the right choice for my companion.

Finally, the movie ended. I breathed a sigh of relief. 'Did you like the film?'

She nodded. 'Thank you.'

I dropped my date back at her home and walked her to the front door, not attempting to kiss her or propose another evening out.

Before leaving, I blurted out, 'Thanks for the wonderful night.'

Once more she nodded and waved the perfume-drenched hanky at me. I escaped before a sneezing fit could commence.

That was the end of Mum's attempts to find me a girl.

No sooner had we settled down in our new home at Canberra, than a co-worker accidentally shot Dad in the leg with a Hilti gun. A nail embedded itself in his tibia.

I wasn't with him at the time of the accident, but when I saw him in hospital, he groaned, 'The pain is worse than my war wound.'

I recalled the lacerations I'd suffered as a child, and my heart went out to Dad in sympathy.

Because the nail proved too dangerous to remove, the surgeon sawed off its protruding end. Dad remained off work for several months and received a handsome sum of money as Workers' Compensation. The money helped furnish our home.

Unable to keep still while on sick leave, he pottered around, digging a vegetable garden and constructing a henhouse. Despite the offending nail in his tibia, Dad's leg healed in time, and he was able to walk without a limp.

At times, recollections of my boyhood came rushing back to me. I recalled combing the sea shore in search of surprises. The long white beach teeming with rock pools. The stranded jellyfish. I missed the sea cadets and the smell of the sea. When folk from my suburb decided to open a Scout Hall, they invited me and four others to train as Scout Masters. Recalling my time as a naval cadet and the joy it had brought me, I consented.

After a period of training, I became a Scout Master and took the boys out camping, instilling in them a love for nature besides teaching them to follow the guide books.

Studies kept me busy and out of mischief. However, I joined my mates at the pub on Friday nights and had a rollicking good time. A friend introduced me to Reg Libbis, who rowed in the Australian Team that came fourth in the Melbourne Olympic Games of 1956.

His powerful grip as he shook hands with me indicated the strength of his biceps. 'Are you interested in rowing?'

'I used to row a bit, back in Portland,' I said. 'I love boating.'

Reg slapped me on my back. 'I'm from Victoria too. Originally from the Albert Park Rowing Club in Melbourne.'

'Reg is a founding member of both the ACT Rowing Association and the Canberra Rowing Club,' my friend added.

Reg chuckled. 'Why not join the Club? I'll coach you on weekends.'

I did not hesitate. *What a chance to be coached by an Olympic rower.* I missed the sea, and love fighting against the elements, but Lake Burley Griffin would do just as well.

Despite the odour of oil and paint that hung about the boat shed, I enjoyed myself. Every morning, I went for a row, and on weekends, I helped repair boats. I took part in races on the lake and my team won several prizes. Exercise kept me lean and fit.

Dave White, a university student who had studied accountancy for two years, needed a break, so he found a job with a builder. We became the best of mates. Dave introduced me to John, a law-graduate whose parents lived in Sydney. We spent weekends at their place—a magnificent building in Palm Beach, overlooking the sand. John's parents resided in a Cape Cod house built against a hill, and John had the top floor all to himself. His room was on the same level as the hill. A stairway from their garden led directly to his room, so we gained access to it without disturbing his parents.

We had our meals with John's family. The Queen had bestowed a knighthood on John's father, but he wore his title with dignity and grace, never treating us like common folk. A quiet soft-spoken man, he drew upon his large hoard of knowledge, dropping little hints on how to make a fortune. I stored his words in my mind, hoping they would come in handy someday.

They proved useful when, years later, I commenced trading on the share market.

Chapter 17

A FEW YEARS AFTER WE had settled down in our own home in Canberra, we visited the Snowy Mountains. The sight of snow was nothing new to my parents, but since I'd left England at the age of two, and had never seen it, my first glimpse of the snow-covered mountains thrilled me. It grew colder as we ascended. We stopped at Thredbo, and I gasped in delight as I breathed in the cold fresh air and we threw snowballs at each other.

Soon the lower halves of our bodies were cold and wet from tramping in the snow.

'It's been so long since I'd been in the snow that I forgot to bring along a change of clothes,' Mum exclaimed.

Dad drove to Jindabyne and we bought socks for ourselves as well as warm leggings for Sally at a local store.

'Take a good look at Jindabyne. She won't be here for long,' the storekeeper said.

It took us only a few minutes to check out the 300-folk town of Jindabyne. I particularly took note of St Columbkille, the lovely Catholic Church. Built mainly of sand and pebbles reclaimed from the Snowy River and mixed with cement, the structure was demolished and relocated to the new township shortly after our visit.

Construction of a dam wall had commenced back in 1949, and on its completion, the old town of Jindabyne was flooded. Farmers who lived in the surrounding area had been forced to give up their large acreages in exchange for a smaller block in the new town.

A few years' later, I drove up to have a look at Lake Jindabyne. The ruins of the Church, which had stood upon a hilltop, is known to the locals as 'Church Island.' It was still visible as a small rocky outcrop. The locals say that most of the trout that inhabit the lake can be found around the site of the old church on Sundays. I chuckled to myself at the thought of church-going trout.

Now, seagulls are the only residents of the island. A chill ran down my spine as I gazed at the remains of the place where so many people had been christened, married and buried, even though all the contents of the graves had been exhumed and interred in new Jindabyne's churchyard. The town retains its sobriquet—an aboriginal name for 'valley.'

Between 1949 and 1974, when the Snowy Mountains Hydro Electric Scheme was completed, over 100,000 men and women from more than 30 countries worked on the scheme. As an apprentice, I met a Swede, who had worked on the same bricklaying team as I did. He had formerly competed in an Olympic Skiing Team.

'Come up to the Snowy,' he said. 'The pay is excellent. I'll coach you in skiing on your days off.'

I asked my dad for his advice. He shook his head. 'You'll be unable to work in winter. The cold freezes everything. It'll be impossible to work. It was the same in England the year we left. I was out of work for months!'

I took his advice and was glad I did. That winter, many of my fellow-apprentices returned to Canberra. They were unable to renew their apprenticeship as they had broken their contract so they hung around, looking for work as labourers.

Even in Canberra, when working outdoors in winter, my left ear suffered from frostbite despite wearing a beanie as it somehow slipped off my ear. Fortunately, I didn't lose my ear, but it is still tender, and extremely sensitive to the sun.

Time passed. I completed my apprenticeship in bricklaying and enrolled in a Clerk of Works degree. Studies kept me inundated amid a cyclone of examinations. I toiled hard and studied hard but work never frightened me.

I loved going to the Bathurst car races—one of the world's top three motor racing circuits. Sometimes, on the way home from college at nights, strangers drove alongside and dared me to a race, but I ignored them. One weekend, however, after attending the races, the longing to race my car intensified, so I accepted their challenges. Canberra was quiet at night in those days and it wasn't too dangerous to take up the gauntlet.

The thrill of the race made me consider rally driving as a sport and I asked for a quote from a mechanic to convert my Datsun into a racing car. The cost was prohibitive, so I decided to wait until I completed my studies and found a position as Clerk of Works or Building Foreman.

One winter day in 1966, an envelope bearing the Commonwealth of Australia emblem arrived, ordering me to present myself before a medical board.

The letter ended with the warning, 'Failure to submit to a medical examination is an offence under the National Services Act.'

In 1964, the government had introduced compulsory National Service for twenty-year-old males. I knew I had to present myself, even though I was a pacifist. In order to be exempted on the basis of conscientious objection, an applicant needed to object to *all* wars, not merely one specific war. I didn't want to plead for an exemption and register as a conscientious objector, and be labelled a coward or a shirker. But I didn't want to fight, to kill.

Providence intervened and prevented me from answering my call up. Next weekend, while skiing at Mt Kosciusko, a sharp sensation shot through my lower back. I drove home, hoping a rub with liniment would fix the problem, but the ache increased.

The next morning, as I opened the door to leave for work, I collapsed to the ground without warning and floundered on the floor in agony.

'Colin,' Mum shouted, and ran towards me.

Dad dropped the work-tools he'd been holding and rushed forward. 'What happened? Have you broken something?' The furrows deepened on his weather-beaten brow.

I shook my head.

Mum's blue eyes filled with tears. She ran off and phoned for an ambulance.

I lay in agony, waiting for the ambos. On their arrival, they lifted me gently and laid me on a stretcher. A wave of pain shot through me as the vehicle screamed to Canberra's only hospital.

I lost consciousness.

When I regained my senses, I was lying on my stomach, unable to move. *So many others have been struck down by polio recently. Do I have polio?* Perspiration beaded my brow. I groaned and dug my face into the pillow.

Someone kept prodding my back. 'Stand.' He tapped me on my shoulder.

I gritted my teeth and tried to get up but collapsed in a heap.

The doctor caught me and helped me back into bed. 'There's an abscess on the sacrum—your lower back. It requires immediate surgery.'

A wave of relief surged through me. *It's* not *polio!*

'But you must realise it has its risks,' he continued. 'Being so close to the nerve centres, there is a possibility of damaging one or more of them. You may never walk again.'

I gasped. *I may end up a cripple and never go bushwalking or boating again!* 'Is there an alternative?'

'If I don't operate, you will get blood poisoning.'

'Then please go ahead. I can't stand this any longer.' I shut my eyes, trying to blot out the waves of pain.

As soon as I signed the consent forms, he performed the operation.

After my operation, even before I opened my eyes, the odour of antiseptic and the stench of something putrid assailed my nostrils. 'What's that smell?' I asked a nurse, who bent down over me.

'That's the puss oozing out from the wound. The surgeon has inserted a tube to drain off the stuff. You had a large boil on your sacrum.'

The pain in my back subsided within a few days and I was able to leave the hospital. The operation resulted in a great wound that took some time to heal and left a deep fissure.

I failed to report to the medical officer, but a Sickness Certificate from the surgeon saved the situation. The Lord had helped me miss my call-up.

I blushed in embarrassment when my friends departed for service overseas to Vietnam.

Two years later, they returned changed men. Some were addicted to drugs; others to alcohol. Another came home sexually inadequate—his marriage in ruins.

I heard about it when his wife said, 'Jacob doesn't sleep with me anymore. I think he's having an affair.'

I gasped and averted my face from them, but later I attempted to speak to him. He confided in me about the medicinal drugs administered to him in Vietnam which had made him impotent.

War takes its toll in many different ways and there's a price to pay for everyone. I shuddered. *Could I have suffered the same fate if the well-timed operation hadn't prevented me from answering my call up?*

Chapter 18

My family had traditional Christmas dinners every year, but Canberra was too hot to endure a steaming dinner of hot roast turkey followed by plum pudding. To avoid such an inappropriate meal for our Australian climate, in the summer holidays, I would pack my camping gear and head off. At times, I went to Sydney—'the Big Smoke', as I called it.

During the Christmas break in my twenty-fourth year, I set off for Adelaide. My intention was to drive via Mildura to Adelaide and see the scenic Barossa Valley with its world-famous wineries, before visiting my childhood friends and favourite places in and around Portland.

At Adelaide, I booked a day-tour of the vineries. To my horror, I was assigned a front seat next to a female. She was petite and had a perm. Like my date at the open-air cinema, she looked the type who would be drowned in perfume. I shrank back at the mere thought of sitting beside her, and sat at the rear of the bus until another passenger arrived.

Five minutes later, someone tapped me on the shoulder. 'Excuse me,' he said. 'I think you're sitting in my place.'

Although tempted to exchange tickets with him, I decided otherwise and moved to another seat. The same thing happened again. I moved from seat to seat. It reminded me of the game, *Musical Chairs*, which we'd played as kids, and felt a hot flush rise to my face.

I returned to my allocated seat when all the back seats filled. The girl next to me smelled like a rose, and fortunately, I didn't get an allergic reaction to her perfume.

When the tour director called out the names on his list of passengers, before departure, I discovered that my companion's name was Hazel. Every so often, the driver would glance at us in the mirror and make some remarks about the scenery through which we were passing, and by the time we'd stopped for lunch, I'd developed a camaraderie with him.

At lunch-time, I joined some fellow tourists at a table, and seeing Hazel heading towards us, my gentlemanly instincts drove me to rise and draw up a chair for her. Her eyes lit up when she smiled and thanked me. She chatted with me during the meal, removing my cloak of bashfulness and leaving me comfortable and relaxed.

When the group stopped at a winery for wine-tasting, she hung around. That suited me, as I knew no one else and only threw occasional remarks into the general tide of conversation.

Towards the end of the tour, the bus driver asked us, 'Have either of you seen the sights of Adelaide? You should see Light's Vision at night. It's a sight not to be missed.'

'I don't know how to get there,' I answered.

Hazel produced a map of Adelaide from her bag and handed it to me.

After perusing it, I plucked up courage and asked, 'Have you been to the Botanical Gardens?'

'No. I haven't.' She smiled. Not a *come-hither* smile, but a half-hesitant, half-open smile that made my heart lurch.

'Would you like to go there? We can drive over in my car. I only took this tour as I wanted to visit the best wineries in the Barossa Valley. We could drop in at the Botanical Gardens first and then go on to Light's Vision.'

Her face lit up. 'I'd love that.'

I arranged to pick her up from her hotel the next morning.

Count Your Blessings

What prompted me to be so reckless? I told myself I was on holiday and could afford a little fun. A hundred different thoughts raced through my mind. *Will she pester me to continue taking her out again? Will she be a hindrance? Perhaps I shouldn't turn up at the hotel?*

But that would be against my principles. I had promised to pick the girl up and will not let her down.

I arrived at the appointed time and drove her to the Botanical Gardens. As we walked, I pointed out to her plants that had been familiar to me. Hazel listened intently as we wandered around in the gardens. I enjoyed myself so much that I didn't notice the time until the light faded and the shadows grew longer and finally disappeared with the setting sun.

Reluctant to leave, we rambled back to the exit but the gates were locked. The sign read: *Gardens closed at 6.00 pm.*

Hazel appeared shocked as she confronted the tightly-secured gate and high stonewall.

'Don't worry,' I said. 'We'll easily get over this.' I pushed through the low shrubs, climbed the wall and pulled her up. I felt her slender waist and soft, warm body in my arms as I lowered her to the pavement.

I'd tried to maintain my protective shell the whole day, but during our time together, it eroded away, and love took possession of me. Previously, we had kept our distance. Now we walked hand-in-hand. Everything seemed different. We strolled along in silence. No words were necessary. Happy, anxious and expectant, I felt as though I'd never truly lived, until now. The soft and languid air, the summer sky lit by countless candles in the firmament, brought a mystique to the evening. I glimpsed the beauty beneath my companion's dusky complexion and tiny stature. A surge of desire tightened my throat. I knew that the flame she lit within me would never die.

I drove to Light's Vision in a daze. We walked up to the top of the hill in silence. Gazing into her eyes on the hilltop, I lost myself, knowing I loved her and wanted her with my entire being. Submerged in a sea of love, I folded her in my arms and kissed her.

She returned my embrace.

A strange destiny had guided us to each other that summer's day in 1969. Breathless, we stood together watching the stars and sharing our dreams. Hazel lived in Perth and was studying for her Bachelor of Arts degree at the University of West Australia. Born in Mandalay, she had migrated to Australia in 1967.

'I've booked a return trip to Perth for tomorrow morning,' she said.

Am I going to lose her? I gasped inwardly. 'Will you write to me when you get back to Perth?' I asked.

'Of course I will.'

We promised to write regularly.

Each week, I wrote on blue note paper and enclosed it in a blue envelope. When Hazel's letters arrived, I found a quiet place in the garden and devoured every word.

My parents were glad I'd finally met someone I liked.

Eight long months passed. They seemed like years. The tree of time shed its leaves too slowly. Overcome with desire to be with Hazel again, I asked Mum whether I could invite her to meet the family, during the autumn break.

'She must be something, if you want to ask her over,' Mum said.

Dad's eyes twinkled. 'Guess it's about time you settled down.'

'Is she English or Australian?' Mum asked.

'She's Eurasian but speaks the Queen's English.'

Dad smiled. A quizzical smile. 'That's more than *we* do.'

Barely able to hide the pride in my voice, I said, 'She's a teacher.'

'Like your cousin Geoff,' Mum said. 'Another teacher in our family!'

Heat rose to my face. 'So, will you welcome her here?'

'Of course, she may stay with us,' Mum said, giving Dad a nudge.

I counted the hours. It snowed in Canberra the day before Hazel arrived, and because it rarely snowed in Canberra, Sally, who was ten at the time, collected a handful of snow and stored it in the fridge for Hazel.

Hazel looked radiantly happy as she fell into my waiting arms at the airport. I drove her to all the beautiful places in Canberra and stopped at the Carillion on Lake Burley Griffin. The trees, clothed in their autumn foliage, lent a perfect setting to our romance.

After a timeless evening, I took her to meet my parents. They welcomed her, and Sally presented her with the now-frozen ball of crushed ice. Hazel's eyes glistened.

A delightful week passed. One evening, we went back to Lake Burley Griffin and walked together hand-in-hand. Trees stood deep in fallen leaves. A breeze sent them scurrying like children hurrying from school. We laughed from sheer delight.

'It's turning a bit chilly,' I said. 'I think we should get into the car.'

I turned on the heater and took Hazel into my arms. Then I proposed to her. I waited breathless. *Will she accept me as her husband?*

She did not keep me in suspense for long. Throwing her arms around me, she whispered the word I'd been waiting for. We remained locked in each other's embrace until darkness set in. A police officer shone his torch on us, only to find Hazel seated on my lap.

The strong flashlight brought us down to earth. Time had flown by on rosy wings, so I turned on the ignition and drove home.

Mum and Dad were still up, watching television, when we returned. They didn't usually stay up so late. Perhaps they guessed I'd be the bearer of good news.

'We're engaged to be married,' I announced, while Hazel hung on my arm and smiled. I felt her hand tremble either from excitement or fear of what my parents would say.

Mum flew from her seat and kissed us. Dad rose, shook hands with me, and kissed Hazel.

'We'll have an engagement party before you fly back to Perth,' Mum said, turning to Hazel. 'I'll hand out the invitations, as there's not much time left before your departure.'

The next day, Mum was as good as her word. She invited all her friends to our engagement party. Among the guests were Reg Libbis, the ex-Olympian, Jim O'Brien, who was later to serve as my Best Man, and several other friends.

'It's the first party I've ever had. I loved it,' Hazel said, when the last guest had gone.

On the day of her departure for Perth, I dropped Hazel off at the airport. I clutched at my throat as the plane took flight. *When will I see her again? How will I live without her?*

I wrote daily. Words welled up within my heart and spilled on the paper. Destined for each other, we were both so much in love.

As soon as I'd completed my studies in the Clerk of Works Diploma, I packed everything into the blue Datsun and drove across the dusty Nullarbor.

Count Your Blessings

Hazel introduced me to her family. Her mother May was a soft-spoken lady, who was so glad that I intended to find a job and settle down in Perth. Hazel's elder brother, Bertie, was in England at the time. Her sister Rose was married to an Irishman, Pat. Winston the youngest scarcely spoke, but he looked at me with curiosity.

During the early seventies, recession gripped Australia in a stranglehold, and I was unsuccessful in securing employment in Perth.

'You lack experience and look too young to be a Clerk of Works,' the manager said, at one of my interviews.

The Builders' Union Rep. shook his head. 'There are no jobs here. Return to Canberra where your job remains open for you.'

I believed a man should provide for his wife and not let her support him, so I asked Hazel if she would accompany me back to Canberra.

'We'll marry as soon as the banns are read,' I said. 'We could live with my parents until our marriage. Then we'll rent a unit in Queanbeyan, just across the border in New South Wales. Accommodation is cheaper there and it's not far from my work.' I saw the struggle in her face. She'd have to give up her good job and her family to be with me.

Fortunately, it was at the end of the academic year, and since we could not part from each other, Hazel agreed to quit her teaching position. We knew there'd be hard work ahead. We had some savings, but not near enough to build our dream home.

I drove back to Canberra via Esperance and Albany. At Esperance, the sea had a pinkish hue, a shade neither of us had ever witnessed in the ocean. I recalled my childish delight when I'd first seen the Blue Lakes in Victoria. Albany's whaling station reminded me of Portland, where pods of whales repeatedly dived close to shore. I shared my cherished memories of Portland with Hazel, promising to take her there one day.

In our joy, the dust of the Nullarbor Plains turned to stardust. We were about to be joined for eternity.

On my return to Canberra, my employer promoted me to a building supervisor's position and I provided for the two of us until Hazel found employment.

Dad and Mum were overjoyed. We stayed at their place for a few months and arranged for our wedding in February.

'I can only marry in a Catholic Church,' Hazel said.

Impressed by her faith, I received instructions from the parish priest and was baptised before the marriage ceremony.

We spent our honeymoon at Wombeyan Caves and slept, surrounded by hills, under a canopy of stars. Our tent excelled any wedding suite at the grandest hotel. Those precious days remain like a mosaic in my memory. We needed no luxuries to make us happy. We had each other. I had staked my liberty when I went into harness and Hazel had risked her entire happiness. The gamble paid off.

Hazel found employment as a kitchen maid scrubbing pots and pans and cleaning the oven at a hotel. She had left an excellent job in Perth at my request. I intended to make it up to her once we had settled down into our new home.

By the end of the year, Hazel was working in the Public Service. We moved into a tiny flat at Queanbeyan and bought a block of land from the government on time-payment. Then we made an application for a government loan.

Called up for an interview, I arrived full of hope.

The clerk eyed us contemptuously. He'd obviously seen many young couples who had also needed help. 'Before we can grant a loan, we need to know how much you earn and what amount of money you have to start with.'

I told him the total amount of our savings.

He shook his head. 'That won't pay for much!'

'I'm a builder. I intend to do most of the work myself. All I need to pay for are the building materials, the roof-tiler, the plumber and the electrician.'

He looked me up and down. 'Well, build your house up to lock-up stage and we'll loan you enough to finish the job. Contact us when that is done, and we'll send someone out to inspect it before we grant you a loan.'

No amount of persuasion would alter his decision. All we had was sufficient to lay the foundations. We were in dire straits.

That night, Hazel and I discussed the situation we were in.

'We have a block of land which we have to pay off month by month. On top of that we have to save sufficient money to buy the bricks and mortar! The money we have now will only be enough to build the foundations. We'll have to wait until I earn enough money to buy the necessary bricks.'

Hazel looked at me aghast. 'I'm in the final year of my B.A, but I'll be reimbursed for my university studies when I've graduated. Perhaps that'll help?'

I nodded. We decided to go ahead and build a house even if it took years. No amount of hardship was too great for us.

In the evenings and on weekends I commenced building our home. In time, I was able to start construction on a solid brick house. My wife helped by mixing the mortar and wheeling the barrow to me.

That same year Hazel completed her studies as an external student, and on her graduation, she was promoted to Graduate Clerk. Her salary increased and she received a refund of her university fees. The cheque gave us enough cash to put a roof over the house and bring it to lock-up stage, thus enabling us to obtain the first instalment of the government loan.

Things moved swiftly after that. We paid for an electrician, plumber and plasterer, and brought our home to near-completion.

The following year, we were thrilled to discover that Hazel was pregnant. She sent away for a 'Baby Bundle' and knitted a little blue outfit for the baby, who was due in September. The Baby Bundle contained every day care items for the new-born, like nappies and vests. She lost no time in enrolling in a pre-natal class where she could learn breathing exercises to help her during the birth of our baby. 'I also need to do a course in cooking,' she said. 'There won't be much time once baby is born. I want a boy—a boy who looks like you.'

I smiled. 'She could be a girl and look like you.'

'My grandmother had twins. Perhaps we'll have twins—a girl and a boy,' Hazel joked.

We bought a large three-roomed tent so that when we went camping our baby could sleep in his own room. The dash to complete things now grew to a frenzy. I rented a house closer to our block of land and toiled on—sometimes even after daylight hours.

At nights, I lay on my back as my life unfolded before me. I had been a young battler and, like most self-made men, I took pride in my obscure beginnings. I visualised my childhood and the ghosts of the past. Grandpa Newton loomed foremost in my mind's eye. I thought about Kacker Duston, standing at the doorway of his shop, the Aboriginal shearer and his dreamtime stories, and the country girl—whose name I'd forgotten—who'd taken me for trips in her old bomb. I recalled my passing fantasies—my childhood dream of living alone on an island, my boyhood-vision of owning a farm like Pa Newton, and the teenage longing to join the Royal Mercantile Navy.

Had I joined, I'd never have met Hazel. Now I'd settled down with a loving wife and I possessed the most precious pearl of all—the gift of faith. Despite all the hardships we had faced as a family, the pain caused by Mum's mood swings and the many reversals of fortune during my younger days, all my dreams were more than satisfied.

I counted my blessings and remained in utter bliss, totally unaware that in marriage one must taste the bitter as well as the sweet. That marriage is not a bed of roses. That disappointments could crush us.

Blinded by love, we looked forward to a life of complete happiness.

THE END

www.ingramcontent.com/pod-product-compliance
Lightning Source LLC
Chambersburg PA
CBHW071626080526
44588CB00010B/1286